AMERICAN
JAZZ
MUSICIANS

Collective Biographies

AMERICAN JAZZ MUSICIANS

Stanley I. Mour

Enslow Publishers, Inc.

44 Fadem Road	PO Box 38
Box 699	Aldershot
Springfield, NJ 07081	Hants GU12 6BP
USA	UK

Library of Congress Cataloging–in–Publication Data

Mour, Stanley I.
    American jazz musicians / Stanley I. Mour.
        p.   cm — (Collective biographies)
    Discography: p. 121
    Includes bibliographical references and index.
    Summary: Profiles ten notable jazz musicians, including Louis Armstrong,
John Coltrane, and Miles Davis.
    ISBN 0–7660–1027–9
    1. Jazz musicians—United States—Biography—Juvenile literature.
[1. Musicians. 2. Jazz.] I. Title. II. Series.
ML3929.M68   1998
781.65'092'273—dc21
    [B]   97–27173
                                                               CIP
                                                            AC MN

Printed in the United States of America

10 9 8 7 6 5 4 3 2 1

Photo Credits: Jazz at Lincoln Center p. 96; Rutgers University Institute of
Jazz Studies pp. 10, 17, 20, 26, 28, 33, 38, 45, 48, 53, 58, 64, 68, 73, 76,
83, 86, 91, 101.

Cover Photo: Rutgers University Institute of Jazz Studies

Contents

Preface

Jazz is America's unique contribution to the world of music. Classical music, the music of Europe, was played only for kings, queens, and the wealthy individuals who supported the musicians and composers. The music of the people was folk songs.

Jazz first started in the American South. Its ancestors are the songs slaves sang to entertain their young and to combat the boredom of picking crops. Gospel, ragtime, and the blues also are related to jazz.

The music we know today as jazz, however, was created in the cities, notably New Orleans and, later, Kansas City and Chicago. It was created mostly by poor African-American men and women. Jazz was played anywhere there was a musician and an instrument. It was heard on the city streets, on riverboats, and in saloons and dance halls.

For many of the musicians who were born into poverty, jazz was more than music. It was a way for them to express their feelings about life and the events around them. And it was also a way for them to make a few dollars. A few individuals even gained fame and wealth by playing jazz.

You are about to take a look at the lives of ten individuals considered to be giants in the world of jazz. As you read about them, you will note that all but one are African Americans. That is because jazz really is the music of black Americans. Of course, there are many excellent white musicians, but jazz owes its existence to African-American musicians.

You will note, too, that nine of the ten artists are male. In the early years, jazz was dominated by males. Female instrumentalists were rare. Most of the female performers who gained recognition were singers. Mary Lou Williams was one exception. Fortunately times have changed and many female jazz instrumentalists are now well known.

As it developed, jazz moved through various stages. This book, as best as possible, presents the musicians in a chronological manner. Ragtime is generally considered the forerunner of modern jazz. The most famous individual in the era of ragtime was Scott Joplin. Ragtime evolved into Dixieland, what today we call New Orleans jazz.

Many early jazz musicians came from New Orleans. Both Louis Armstrong and Wynton Marsalis began their careers there. Although few musicians have reached the level of success and fame of Armstrong and Marsalis, you still can hear many outstanding jazz bands and musicians in New Orleans.

In the thirties and forties, jazz moved into another phase known as the era of the big bands. During this period the music was written and arranged for big bands like those of Duke Ellington, Benny Goodman, and others. Through their many tours, their music was heard around the globe. During the 1930s and 1940s, jazz also gained respectability among the young middle classes of both races. It was no longer thought of as music for "low-class people."

Following World War II, the big bands began to disappear and small musical groups became popular. Another phase of jazz had arrived. It was called bebop. The bebop movement was led by Dizzy Gillespie and Charlie "Bird" Parker.

Out of bebop came the "cool jazz" movement, led by Gil Evans, Claude Thornhill, and Miles Davis. Davis was also present at the birth of "free jazz" and "fusion," two more phases in the development of jazz.

Bebop evolved into hard bop, and then, led by John Coltrane, that music evolved into cool jazz. Today, jazz is in a period known as classicism. One of the leaders of this movement is Wynton Marsalis. Apparently he is trying to return jazz to its original roots.

Just where jazz is going, probably no one, including the musicians who play it, knows. There is no doubt, however, that it will continue to change. Musicians will come and go as they always have. And as always, each will make a unique contribution that will help change jazz. Another thing is also certain. Jazz, though it will be played around the globe, will always be America's music.

Scott Joplin

Scott Joplin

"King of Ragtime"

To understand Scott Joplin, one needs to understand what life was like for a person of color following the Civil War. The war had ended slavery. Yet those who had been slaves remained poor, and because they owned no land, they had to farm for others. Most over the age of ten could not read or write,[1] so they weren't prepared to take jobs that required those skills. In the cities, many of the factory jobs that required no reading and writing skills were being taken by immigrant whites from Europe. Life for the newly freed slave was very difficult.

In the South, where African Americans were treated especially harshly, achievements by them were not considered newsworthy. The birth of an African-American child was not considered important enough to be entered in any public record. It is not surprising, then, that information about Scott Joplin's life is incomplete, confusing, and puzzling.

Scott was born on November 24, 1868. One writer claims he was born "in the piney woods of Texas."[2] Another says it was Texarkana, Texas.[3] Still a third says no records of his birth exist.[4]

Scott's father, Jiles (or Giles), farmed as a slave, but when he was freed, he moved to Texarkana to work as a laborer on the railroad. He had played violin in a plantation dance band and wanted his family to have an interest in music.

Scott's mother, Florence Givens,[5] helped develop a family musical tradition through playing the banjo and singing. Each child played a stringed instrument or sang.[6]

There are two versions about how Scott's musical career began. In one, Mrs. Joplin, a servant for a white family, took young Scott to work with her. The family had a piano, which Scott was allowed to play.[7] According to the second version, Scott discovered a piano at a neighbor's house and began to putter around with it. When Jiles realized his son had a real talent for the piano, he bought him an old used one.[8]

Whichever version is accurate, Scott started to play the piano. By the time he was eleven, he was an excellent pianist. He experimented with the instrument for a while. Then a local music teacher happened to hear him.[9] He was so impressed that he offered Scott free lessons.[10]

His teacher was a graduate of a German university and was well educated. He introduced Scott to the music of many classical composers. Scott decided music would be his life's work. He dreamed of three things. First was to make a good living. Second was to become famous. Third was to help make ragtime acceptable to the world.

When Scott told his father he wanted to become a musician, his father did not understand. He believed Scott should go to work and help the family. They argued and fought. Scott decided to leave home. When his mother died, he left. No one is sure how old he was then,[11] but he was probably around fourteen.

Scott roamed the area, playing in various towns in Texas and Louisiana and up and down the Mississippi River. Jobs were easy for him to find. He played in gambling halls, cafés, and saloons. He worked anywhere he could earn money.

After traveling around for several years, he made St. Louis his base of operation. St. Louis had a lot of bars and saloons where he could listen to other musicians. And there were many small towns surrounding St. Louis where Scott could also play.

According to some writers, Scott visited the Chicago World's Fair in 1893.[12] There is no evidence that he played at the fair.[13] He most likely played in some of the many places that had opened to attract fairgoers.

He is believed to have met Oris Saunders in Chicago.[14] Saunders, who was from Sedalia, Missouri, believed Scott was a musical genius.[15] He became Joplin's unofficial manager. When the fair closed, the two went to Sedalia.[16]

Sedalia was a decent place despite being segregated. The African-American schools were adequate, and there were several African-American newspapers.[17] There were clubs and saloons where an African-American musician could find plenty of work. Sedalia even had a music school.[18] Scott enrolled there to further his study of music.

To support himself, he played in clubs—in the white clubs for money, in the African-American clubs for fun.[19] Early in 1896, ragtime, called jig piano,[20] was introduced in New York. Ragtime, "ragged time," is a complex type of piano music. It is based on classical music but has an African rhythm.[21] Ragtime also drew from German and Italian marching music.[22] It is not improvised music. It is composed. It has been described as "white music, played black."[23]

Joplin was fascinated by rag and focused his attention on composing and playing it. In 1898 he completed the "Maple Leaf Rag." It was published by John Stark, who owned a music store and publishing company in Sedalia. How Stark came to publish the song depends on which version of the story you believe.

According to one version, Stark passed the Maple Leaf Club one day and heard Joplin playing in a back room. He asked him to come by his music store the next day. When Joplin appeared, he had a small boy with him who danced while he played.[24] No one knows why Joplin brought the boy. Whatever the reason, Stark agreed to publish the song.

In the other version of their meeting, Stark did not go to the club at all. Joplin simply appeared at the store with the child. The rest of the story is the same. The child danced while Scott played, and Stark bought the song.[25]

Stark and Joplin formed a partnership. The sheet music did not sell well at first. When it finally caught on about six months after it was published, seventy-five thousand copies were sold.[26] Not too long after that, sales reached 1 million copies. In time, the song made both Stark and Joplin wealthy. Joplin had achieved the first part of his dream. He was indeed making a good living.

Joplin no longer had to play in clubs. He could devote most of his time to composing and teaching, and he became a local celebrity. He married Belle Hayden, the sister-in-law of a friend. In late 1900 or early 1901, they moved to St. Louis, where Stark had gone to live.[27]

Joplin believed that ragtime should be more than just piano music. He started working on a ragtime ballet and a ragtime opera. John Stark, though, believed ragtime was merely popular music and should remain so. To Joplin's disappointment, Stark would not provide the money to stage his ballet *The Ragtime Dance* or his ragtime opera *A Guest of Honor.*

The relationship between Joplin and Stark cooled. Joplin began taking his music to other publishers. He was still composing ragtime songs, but he had become obsessed with writing a ragtime opera. He was also beginning to have emotional and mental problems. And his marriage was coming to an end.

From 1903 to 1905, Joplin did not produce much and was beginning to believe he had lost his ability to compose. Slowly, though, he began composing and publishing again. He went to New York, where he met Lottie Stokes. She was interested in Scott's music. Soon Lottie became the second Mrs. Joplin. They bought a house. Scott had his studio in one part of the house, and in the other part Lottie ran a boardinghouse for actors and musicians.

At last Joplin completed his second opera, *Treemonisha,* the story of a young African-American woman who led her people out of ignorance and superstition.[28] Joplin called it a folk opera rather than a ragtime opera, but there was no interest in publishing or staging it. He did not give up. Getting *Treemonisha* staged became the focus of his life and work.

Unable to find someone to stage *Treemonisha,* he decided to do it himself. He rented a theater and hired a cast. There was no money for scenery, costumes, or musicians, so the opera was performed on a bare stage with Scott playing the music on the

Scott Joplin on the cover of a November 1947 issue of *Jazz Record.*

piano.[29] The performance, before an audience of invited friends, was a miserable failure.[30]

Scott was deeply disturbed. He did not write much. He and Lottie lived on what she made renting rooms in the house and on what he earned by teaching. But he was depressed and ill. He lacked interest in what he was doing and worked only irregularly.

Once again he was showing signs of mental problems. He started to neglect his students, and finally they stopped coming to him. His physical agility was failing, and he was having trouble recognizing friends.

On February 5, 1917, gravely ill, he was admitted to the hospital. Not quite two months later, on April 1, Scott Joplin died. He was forty-nine. His physician said his death was the result of complications from a venereal disease. But those who knew him said he never got over his failure to have his opera staged. *Treemonisha* had broken Scott Joplin's heart.

The ragtime craze faded with Joplin's death. For more than fifty years, rag music was ignored by musicians and by the public. Then in 1972, Scott Joplin was reintroduced to the world as a result of the movie *The Sting*. The film, starring Paul Newman and Robert Redford, featured two of Scott's greatest songs, the "Maple Leaf Rag" and "The Entertainer." Ragtime became popular once again. Scott Joplin had achieved the second and third parts of his dream. He had become known around the world, and ragtime music had become respectable.

Daniel Louis Armstrong

"Satchmo"

No one is exactly sure when Louis Armstrong was born. One writer gives 1898 as the year;[1] another says 1900;[2] and a third claims 1901.[3] Armstrong himself said he was born on July 4, 1900,[4] but according to an article in *Newsweek* magazine,[5] a baptismal certificate that was found in the 1980s proves that his actual date of birth was August 4, 1901. Whatever doubts there are about his birth date, however, no one ever questioned his ability to play jazz. And there is no doubt that Armstrong had a tremendous influence on all jazz trumpeters who came after him. Even today, many trumpet players admit that they patterned their playing after that of Louis.

Daniel Louis Armstrong

Louis was born in a run-down cabin in a New Orleans, Louisiana, slum. His mother, who was fifteen when he was born, was the granddaughter of slaves. Soon after Louis was born, his father left the family, and the boy was sent to live with his father's parents.

A few years later, Louis was sent to live with his mother. They were very poor. Most days they didn't have enough food. Louis often had to hunt through garbage cans for something to eat.[6] At times he had to wear rags because he didn't have any decent clothes.

No one cared whether Louis attended school, so he spent most of his time wandering the streets, singing for food and the few pennies people gave him. Sometimes he sang alone, sometimes with a group. It was his first experience with music.

When he was about thirteen, he was arrested. It may have been because he fired his mother's gun in the street to welcome the new year.[7] Or it may have been because he was getting into trouble roaming the streets.[8] Whatever the reason, his arrest probably was a blessing. Had he not been arrested, he might not have had a musical career.

Louis was sent to the Colored Waifs Home for Boys, a juvenile detention center. His life there was better than his life at home had been. He had enough food to eat and suitable clothing.

He sang in the home's choir, but he really wanted to play in the brass band. The band played all kinds

21

of music, and Louis loved it. One day he asked the band director if he could join the band. He seemed so excited about joining that the director gave him a battered cornet, a trumpetlike instrument, and started to teach Louis to play. It was then that Louis decided he would become a musician.

Louis was a shy, easygoing person. He seemed to work best when pushed and supported by very strong people. Joe "King" Oliver was such a person. Louis met Oliver after he was released from the home. Oliver, who played cornet in Edward "Kid" Ory's jazz band, realized the youngster could play well. He began to help Louis find jobs playing in the area.

Louis had an excellent ear for music and learned quickly. Though much younger, he could play as well as most of the other musicians. He played so well that in 1918, when Oliver left for Chicago, Louis took his place in Ory's band.

The band played in clubs around New Orleans and on riverboats, which were like floating dance halls.[9] The boats traveled from town to town up and down the Mississippi River. Louis played in Fate Marable's Band, which traveled aboard the *Sidney*. Playing on the river excursion steamers gave Louis the opportunity to play before all kinds of people. He became a better musician and even learned to read music a little.

In 1922 King Oliver invited Armstrong to come to Chicago and play in his band. It was during his stay with Oliver that Armstrong made some records. Other musicians heard him and were impressed by his ability. He was soon known to many musicians around the country.

While playing with Oliver, Louis met Lillian "Lil" Hardin, the pianist with the band. She and Louis fell in love, and in 1924, Lil became the second Mrs. Armstrong (Louis had been married briefly in 1918). Louis would have two more marriages.

Lil, too, was a strong person. She encouraged Louis to leave Oliver and join Fletcher Henderson, who led one of the best bands, African-American or white, in the business. Louis took her advice, and in 1924 he went to New York to play with Henderson.

Henderson was an accomplished musician and arranger. While with him, Armstrong met and played with some white musicians, whose style of playing was quite different from his. They learned from each other.

After a little over a year, Armstrong became tired of being away from home, and he missed Lil. He returned to Chicago and joined her and the band she had started.

Not an idle person, Armstrong obtained a record contract. His group, the Hot Five, consisted of Louis (now playing trumpet), Lil (piano), Kid Ory (trombone), Johnny Dodd (clarinet), and Johnny St. Cyr (banjo). On one of the records, "Heebie Jeebies," Louis sang scat style, which is wordless singing.

During this period, Louis also played with Erskine Tate, who led a symphonic jazz orchestra. He learned to read music better and to play some classical music.

One of the most important years in Armstrong's career was 1929. That year he returned to New York and starred in *Hot Chocolates*, a musical. One of the songs he sang was "Ain't Misbehavin'," written by Thomas "Fats" Waller. This marked the point in Armstrong's career when he began to sing and play popular songs rather than blues music.

Armstrong left the show and went on tour. The tour ended in California, where he decided to stay. By this time he was a nationwide star. He remained in California for about a year. When he returned to Chicago, he formed still another new band.

In 1931 he took the band to New Orleans. It was his first visit to his home city in nine years. While there he was a guest on a radio show. He had to introduce himself because the white announcer wouldn't introduce a black man.

Armstrong was nicknamed Satchelmouth, a person with a big mouth or a person who talks a lot. While he was on his first overseas tour in 1932, an English writer confused the name and called him Satchmo.[10] From that time on, he was "Satchmo" to his fans.

He returned from his long tour of Europe in 1935. The following year, 1936, he made the movie *Pennies From Heaven* with Bing Crosby. He was one

24

of the first African Americans to have more than a bit part in a movie.[11] He then became known much more for his singing and entertaining than he was for his trumpet skills.

In the 1940s, "Pops," as he was called by other musicians, won most of the jazz polls. He won the first *Esquire* magazine poll, then considered to be the most important jazz award of all.

The big band era was ending, so Satchmo started to play only with small groups. One of those groups, "The All-Stars," was the first jazz group to play in Metropolitan Opera Hall in New York, America's most famous opera house.

People came to see Armstrong. It didn't matter where he played or with which group of musicians. The public wanted to see and hear Satchmo sing and play. When crowds heard the first notes of "Sleepy Time Down South," Louis's theme song, they went wild with excitement.

By 1950, Satchmo was probably the best-known entertainer in the world. His face and gravelly voice were known to millions around the world. He made many movies both in this country and in Europe. He was featured on radio and television. He played in jazz festivals everywhere. Because of his popularity, he toured Europe and Asia as a "roving ambassador" for the State Department. Armstrong made appearances with most of the great musicians and entertainers of his time. No matter with whom he appeared, it was always Armstrong the crowd

One of the best-known entertainers of his time, Armstrong was an inspiration to many young musicians.

screamed for most. He became known as America's ambassador of jazz.[12]

During the civil rights marches in the 1960s, Armstrong was criticized by young militant African-Americans. They said he was not involved enough in the marches and struggles of the civil rights movement. But Louis was not a political person. He just wanted to entertain people. He was hurt by the comments.

Armstrong did fight for rights for African Americans, but he did it in his own quiet and dignified way. He even stopped touring for the government because of the way African Americans were treated.

Armstrong was still popular. His recording of "Hello Dolly" was the best-selling single record of 1964. It replaced the Beatles at the top of the record-selling charts.

The tours and long hours Armstrong worked tired him. His health began to fail. He began to perform less and less, but he wouldn't quit. He played as much as his health would permit. On July 4, 1971, he celebrated his seventy-first birthday. Two days later he had a heart attack and died.

When Bing Crosby learned that Satchmo had died, he said, "He was the only musician who ever lived who can't be replaced by someone."[13]

Louis Armstrong had touched the world.

Edward Kennedy Ellington

Edward Kennedy Ellington

"Duke"

He was a band leader, composer, pianist. He was honored by two U.S. presidents and was presented awards from governments around the globe. He played before kings, queens, and common people. He never graduated from high school, but universities gave him honorary degrees. And when he died, he was mourned by millions. Wynton Marsalis, a superb musician himself, said, "Duke Ellington touched more people than confetti."[1]

Edward Kennedy Ellington came into the world on April 29, 1899, in Washington, D.C. He was the son of Daisy Kennedy and James Edward "J.E." Ellington. J.E. worked as a butler for a wealthy physician and sometimes at the White House.[2]

Although not wealthy, the Ellingtons were financially comfortable.

Daisy Ellington smothered her son with love and attention and constantly told him he was "blessed."[3] She wanted him to be a gentleman. According to Duke, his mother taught him that "proper speech and good manners were our first obligations."[4] He had a brother and sister, but Edward apparently was his mother's favorite.

Edward loved baseball. One day he got whacked with a bat. Daisy was watching and immediately decided that her son should engage in gentler activities.[5] Shortly afterward, young Edward started piano lessons.[6]

Both Daisy and J.E. played piano. During Edward's youth, Washington's African-American community offered many different musical experiences for young and old.[7]

About the time Edward entered junior high, a friend started calling him Duke. It was a name that would stick with him his entire life.[8] The same friend set him up to play piano at several parties. He was not an accomplished player, but he could play well enough to entertain. He also learned that there was always a pretty girl hanging around the piano. Duke liked that.

Duke began sneaking into a local burlesque theater.[9] There he heard new piano styles, which years later he would incorporate into his own music. He also started going to the local pool room. Pool rooms in the African-American community were like social clubs where doctors, lawyers, and bankers went to relax. Musicians, too, frequented pool rooms, which contained a piano and other musical instruments. Duke met a lot of important people in such places. Some of the musicians helped him with his piano technique. Some became his partners in his early bands.[10]

Duke was a smart businessman even as a high school youngster. He quickly learned he could make more money booking dates for other bands than playing himself, so he became the agent for several groups.

Duke really wanted to be an artist. And because of his love for drawing, he opened his own sign-painting business while still in high school. During his senior year, he won a poster contest.[11] The prize was a scholarship to study art in New York.[12] Duke didn't accept the scholarship for two reasons. First, he did not wish to go to New York. Second, during the summer of 1918, he and Edna Thompson, a school-mate and neighbor, were married. She was expecting a child. Duke simply could not afford to give up the money he was making in order to attend art school.

In 1923 Duke and four others formed a group called The Washingtonians and went to New York City, where they had no success at all. They often had so little money they would split a hot dog five ways to keep from starving.[13] The band returned to Washington within six months.

But they didn't quit. In 1926 they tried New York again, with Duke as the leader. About this time, too, Duke met Irving Mills, a clever, ambitious music publisher. Mills became agent for the band and acquired a record contract for them.

Things started to get better for Ellington and the band. They were asked to play at the Cotton Club, a very famous nightclub in New York City. While at the Cotton Club, Duke composed and arranged music. They stayed at the club for five years. Five or six nights a week, they played over the radio[14] and became well known across the nation.

In 1933 Mills arranged for Duke to play in London at the Palladium, the best-known variety theater in the world. That same year Duke lectured at New York University.[15] Then, from 1934 to 1939, the band toured the entire United States. The relationship between Duke and Mills was paying off.

Music became the most important thing in Ellington's life. When he wrote his autobiography, he titled it *Music Is My Mistress*.

Ellington's band was unique. It really was more than just a swing band. The men could not only play dance music, but also complex concert numbers. Their performances were similar to those of symphony orchestras. The compositions, many of them written by Ellington, were so personalized that they didn't sound the same when other bands played them.

Ellington not only played the piano, but also composed and arranged music.

But Duke was not a typical bandleader. His players were allowed to participate in all decisions regarding the band. And unlike other leaders, Duke never featured himself as the only soloist. He shared the spotlight.[16] Apparently his approach worked. Many of the members of his band stayed with him for most of their careers. One musician, Harry Carney, was seventeen when he joined the band in 1927 and was still a band member when Duke died.

He was not a typical composer either. His music was written in airports while waiting for planes, in restaurants, or in the backseat of a car while Carney drove him to concerts.

Duke and the band performed each year from 1943 to 1948 at Carnegie Hall. It was another step in the acceptance by the public of jazz and of African-American jazz artists. In 1958, Duke and Ella Fitzgerald, one of the great jazz singers, appeared at Carnegie Hall. Duke also appeared in concert at the Metropolitan Opera House. At each of these concerts, a new Ellington composition was introduced.[17]

Much of Ellington's music reflected his pride in being African American. He wrote "Sepia Panorama, Portrait of Bert Williams," a musical tribute to a popular African-American entertainer. "Creole Love Call" was his first composition to use the human voice as an instrument. "Mood Indigo" is a bluesy type of song, and "Black, Brown and Beige" is a musical painting of the history of African Americans.[18]

Toward the end of World War II, the trend was for smaller groups. Ellington's popularity in this country started to fade. Thirteen tours of Europe from 1950 to 1973, however, indicated he was still popular overseas.

In 1956 Duke Ellington appeared at the Newport Jazz Festival, where the crowds were usually enthusiastic but not rowdy. When he started to play, the crowd became excited. Then Paul Gonsalves, Duke's young tenor sax player, stood and played twenty-seven straight choruses of a song, and the crowd exploded. According to one music critic, it was the longest tenor sax solo ever recorded.[19] The audience screamed and cheered and danced in the aisles. Duke Ellington had returned.

During the sixties, Ellington toured the Middle East and India. He also made trips to Japan, West Africa, and South America. Even after he turned seventy, he still kept on touring. He played in Japan and Australia and the Soviet Union, now Russia.

Ellington was a very private person. Few people knew much about his personal life. He never explained his side when criticized.[20] He completely avoided those subjects he didn't wish to discuss. Still, during the civil rights struggles of the 1960s, he took a public stand on the treatment of African Americans. After a concert in Baltimore he went to eat at a café where African-American students had been refused service. Ellington also was refused service, but the story made the newspapers.[21]

Ellington refused to play a concert in Little Rock, Arkansas, after he learned that African-Americans and whites could not sit together. The following two nights he played in Dallas and Houston but only after being promised that the audiences would not be separated.[22]

Ellington had been raised in a religious home, and he liked church music. It was not surprising, then, that he turned to sacred music as his newest challenge. On September 16, 1965, Duke Ellington presented his first concert of sacred music in Grace Cathedral in San Francisco. The event made the newspapers across the country.[23]

Many people were shocked. Although jazz has some of its roots in hymns, spirituals, and gospel songs, many culturally conservative people still looked upon jazz as "the devil's music."[24] They did not think a jazz musician should be playing in church. The concert, however, was a success, and it was repeated in a number of churches across the country.

On his seventieth birthday, Ellington was honored at the White House and presented the Presidential Medal of Honor, the highest honor a nonmilitary person can receive.[25]

Over the years, Ellington received many honors and awards. *Down Beat* magazine named him to its Jazz Hall of Fame in 1956. In 1971 he was the first jazz musician named to the Royal Academy of Music in Stockholm, Sweden.[26]

On May 24, 1974, shortly after celebrating his seventy-fifth birthday, Duke Ellington died. More than twelve thousand people attended his funeral in New York. The man who really wanted to be an artist probably was the most important composer in jazz history.[27] But in a sense he really was an artist, also. His pictures were created with musical notes rather than with paint.

Mary Lou Williams

4

Mary Lou Williams

"First Lady of Jazz"

Jazz is an art form that has been dominated almost exclusively by males. Many jazz groups were like clubs for men only. Women did find a place in the early days of jazz, but mostly as singers. A few, such as Lil Hardin, Marian McPartland, Hazel Scott, Lovey Austin, and Mary Lou Williams, made names for themselves as pianists.[1] They were excellent musicians. Given the times, however, women were not often given the same opportunities as their male counterparts.

This male-dominated world was the environment in which Mary Lou Williams lived and worked. She believed in herself and in her ability to play. It was these two traits, and her concern for others, that earned her the respect and admiration of her peers.

Mary Elfrieda Scruggs Burley was born in Atlanta, Georgia, on May 8, 1910. When she was very young, the family moved to Pittsburgh. She never knew her father,[2] and apparently nothing is known about him. She never talked about him. She was, however, very fond of her mother, stepfather, and older sister. These were the people she mentioned.

When Mary was around four, she started picking out tunes on the piano. Her mother was an organist. Although she encouraged Mary, she wouldn't give her piano lessons.[3] When her mother was young she had taken lessons, and as an adult she was unable to play without sheet (or written) music. She wanted her daughter to be able to create and improvise as well as read music.

Mary was blessed with a phenomenal memory. And she heard pitch perfectly. Without any difficulty at all, she could identify any note or key by ear. When her third-grade teacher hummed a song one day, Mary told her she knew the key. The teacher didn't believe her. To test her, the teacher played a note on the piano. To the teacher's shock and surprise, Mary identified it.[4]

Mary was very fond of Fletcher Burley, her stepfather. She even took his name. He was a professional gambler, but he liked music. He would sing blues music to her.[5] When he went to gamble, he would take Mary with him. Most places had an upright piano. He would put Mary on a stool, where she would sit and play while he gambled.

Mary started collecting tips when her stepfather passed the hat.[6] When she was a little bit older, she started playing at house parties, for which she received money.

Mary had no formal training, but she listened carefully to all the jazz pianists. Many, particularly Earl "Fatha" Hines and "Jelly Roll" Morton, influenced her.[7] She was especially impressed with Lovey Austin, a female piano player, arranger, and composer. Austin was director at Chicago's Monogram Theater.[8] Mary had heard her when she went to Pittsburgh once.

By the time Mary entered high school, she was quite good on the piano. While still a high school student, a stage show, *Hits and Bits*, came to town. The show's manager advertised for a piano player, and when he heard Mary play, he hired her. When the show ended and was ready to leave town, the manager asked Mary to go with it. Her mother gave permission for Mary to go, but she arranged to have someone travel with her.[9]

While the show was playing in Chicago, Mary met a young musician named John Williams. He had his own band, and on a couple of occasions he asked Mary to play with his group.[10]

When the show's tour ended, Mary returned to Pittsburgh to finish school. Shortly after she returned, her stepfather became ill and was unable to work. Mary became the sole support of the family by playing.[11]

When she finished high school, she joined John Williams and his band for a tour. While in Memphis, his hometown, they were married. It was 1927, and Mary was seventeen years old.

The couple stayed in Memphis and formed a band. Mary played piano and wrote some of the arrangements. John left to join Andy Kirk's band, called Twelve Clouds of Joy, in Oklahoma City. Mary had to remain in Memphis to finish their contract. She then joined John in Oklahoma City.

Mary became deputy director of Twelve Clouds of Joy. She didn't play with the band, but she did write some of the musical arrangements. She remained in that status for about two years. Finally, she became a regular band member.[12] Some critics believed that much of the band's success was due to her arrangements, compositions, and solos.[13]

Mary had to return to Pittsburgh for her stepfather's funeral. While she was there, Kirk's band moved to Kansas City. She rejoined the band there but did more arranging than playing. The band went on a tour that ended in New York.

In Chicago in 1931, while on tour, Mary cut her first record. When the recording session was over, an agent said she needed a better middle name, so he added the Lou.[14] Mary returned to Kansas City after the tour as Mary Lou Williams. She would be known by that name the rest of her life.

When the band played in Cleveland, it was featured on a radio broadcast. Probably as a result of the broadcast, the band was booked into the Apollo Theater in New York City.[15] The Apollo was the place every African-American artist dreamed of playing.

While in New York, Mary Lou started writing musical arrangements for other bands.[16] She didn't make a lot of money, but her name was becoming well known. She wrote for Benny Goodman, who at the time was the biggest name in swing music. She also wrote for Tommy Dorsey and Earl Hines.[17]

The band was booked to play at the Cotton Club in Harlem, once New York's most famous nightclub. At that time, however, a new era in music was beginning and the life of the Cotton Club was about to end.[18] So was Mary Lou's marriage with John Williams.

Unhappy and upset over the breakup of her marriage, Mary Lou quit Kirk's band and returned to Pittsburgh. There she and Harold "Shorty" Baker, a trumpeter, formed their own group. Shortly afterward, Baker left. Mary Lou remained in Pittsburgh for a time, but then she, too, left and joined Baker, who by this time was playing with Duke Ellington.

Mary Lou Williams wrote arrangements for Duke Ellington. She also composed "Trumpet No End" for him. And she composed music for just herself. She performed part of her composition "Zodiac

43

Suite" with the New York Philharmonic Orchestra at Carnegie Hall in 1946.[19]

She tired of the band business and worked for a time as a solo act. She then turned her attention and efforts to bebop, the "new jazz." She was one of the few older musicians who adjusted to bebop. She defended the younger musicians who wanted to play the new jazz.[20] She guided them and worked with them. Her home in New York became a gathering place for young musicians. Sometimes they jammed all night. Sometimes they just talked music. Williams was very helpful to the careers of numerous young musicians.[21] She developed a very close friendship with Dizzy Gillespie and his wife and did some arranging for Gillespie's big band. She also continued to do solo work on occasion.

In 1952, Williams decided to move to Europe. Two years later, in 1954, she returned to New York and, to everyone's surprise, announced she was retiring from music.[22]

Always a religious person, Williams devoted herself to church work and to working with various church charities. Through her involvement with the church, she met Father Peter O'Brien, a Jesuit priest. With his guidance and support, she converted to the Roman Catholic faith. She continued to compose music, but it was church music, not jazz.

Williams established a foundation to help needy musicians and named it Bel Canto, which is Italian for "beautiful singing."[23]

Williams was one of the few older musicians who adjusted to bebop when it became popular.

Father O'Brien urged Williams to resume her career in jazz, and in 1957 she did.[24] With the priest as her manager and press agent, she appeared with Dizzy Gillespie at the Newport Jazz Festival.[25]

In 1969 she composed "Mary Lou's Mass," a work that was commissioned by the Vatican. A year later she adapted the piece for the Alvin Ailey dance troupe.

When Williams came out of retirement, she had a mission. That mission was to "save" jazz.[26] She wanted to revive the values found in the origins of jazz, and to that end she recorded her "History of Jazz."[27] In addition to various awards and honorary degrees she received, in 1977 she became artist-in-residence at Duke University.[28] Williams wrote, performed, lectured, and taught. When her residency ended, she remained at Duke teaching jazz history.

On May 28, 1981, at age seventy-one, Mary Lou Williams died of cancer.

Mary Lou Williams once said, "Anything you are shows up in your music—jazz is whatever you are, playing yourself, being yourself, letting your thoughts come through."[29] Her music reflected her beliefs—her deep feelings about religion, her ability to inspire others, and her desire to help others. Mary Lou Williams has been called "the first woman instrumentalist in jazz."[30] But she wasn't just a female jazz instrumentalist.

She was a jazz great. She was an artist.

Benjamin David Goodman

"The King of Swing"

Young boys like different things. Some are crazy about baseball. Others like to read. Some collect coins or stamps. For Benny Goodman, though, music was his number one interest. When other boys talked about becoming great athletes, Benny talked about becoming a great musician.

Benny's parents, David and Dora Rezinsky Goodman, were Jews who left Russia because Jews were so mistreated there. They settled in a poor neighborhood in Chicago. On May 30, 1909, Benjamin David Goodman was born. He was the eighth of eleven children.

Benjamin was a quiet, thoughtful child who wanted to play music, but the family couldn't afford to buy an instrument for him or pay for music

Benjamin David Goodman

lessons. His father learned about a free music program at a local synagogue and enrolled Benny.[1] There the boy was given a clarinet and started his music lessons.

Benny advanced quickly. Soon the teacher at the synagogue could teach him no more. He sent Benny to Hull House, a social service agency. There the boy studied with a professor from the Chicago Musical College.[2]

Benny loved jazz, the music played mostly by African-American musicians.[3] His teacher hated it and all other popular music. Benny was taught classical music. By age ten he was an accomplished musician.

Benny made his professional debut at age eleven. He played in a theater band wearing shorts, the clothing typical of boys his age. When he was twelve, and wearing shorts, he appeared on stage impersonating Ted Lewis, a famous clarinet-playing showman of the day. He continued wearing shorts until he was into his late teens. Musicians said he had one of the most famous pairs of knees in the music business.[4]

In addition to the African-American jazz musicians he heard, Benny's playing was influenced by a group of young Chicago musicians, the Austin High Gang. They were considered to be the first white players around the area who played in the style of African-American jazz musicians.[5] Benny watched them closely. He listened to everything they did and tried to model his playing after theirs.

In 1925, at age sixteen, Benny joined Ben Pollock's band. When the band wasn't working, he spent the time learning to improvise, creating music as he played. He played with musicians from various musical groups, including his friends from the Austin High Gang. Much of the music was Dixieland, the musical style of New Orleans. This helped Benny learn some of the more difficult techniques of playing jazz.

In 1928 Benny went to New York with the Pollock band. He was nineteen. It wasn't a good time for moving. The country was entering the Great Depression, a period of severe economic hardship, poverty, and high unemployment. There were many musicians but few jobs.

Because of his musical talent, Goodman always managed to find work. He joined a theater band, but he desired to lead his own group. Finally, in 1934, with the help of John Hammond, a wealthy jazz enthusiast and friend, Goodman formed his first band.

This band was "competent if unexciting."[6] It had some talented musicians, but people couldn't dance to the music. The man who hired them for their first engagement was enraged when he realized the customers didn't like the band. He fired the band on the first night of its first job![7]

Goodman was very discouraged. He thought going on a tour might help. In Denver, the first stop, the people didn't like his music any better than those in New York had. He was ready to quit but went on to play in Oakland, California. To his great surprise and delight, the crowds liked the music. Encouraged, Goodman and the band finished the tour at the Palomar Ballroom in Los Angeles, where the dancers went wild over his music.[8] It was the beginning of the era of swing.

Swing is best described as a type of early jazz, or the music of the big bands of the 1920s and 1930s. Like all music, it contains rhythm, melody, harmony, and tone.[9] But swing has written music; early jazz was improvised and usually unwritten. It had to be, since most of the early jazz musicians did not have much formal musical education and could not read music. Swing, unlike much early jazz (ragtime being the exception), is played in a smooth, danceable manner.[10] And because improvising is much more difficult in a big band than in a small group, swing is more structured than improvised music.

Goodman and the band returned to Chicago to play at a hotel for three weeks. They were so popular they stayed eight months. During this time, Goodman and the band were heard on a radio program and began a Sunday concert series.

At one of the concerts, Benny presented the Goodman Trio. The trio consisted of Goodman, Gene Krupa, the drummer from the big band, and Teddy Wilson, a young piano player. Teddy Wilson was an African American.

African-American musicians were not treated well in those days and were not permitted to play in public with white musicians. A few years earlier, in 1931, Earl Hines and his band were forced to walk in the streets of Fort Lauderdale, Florida. They were not permitted to walk on the sidewalks because they were African Americans.[11]

When Benny Goodman included Wilson in the trio, it was the first step toward the public integration of African-American and white musicians. It was a significant event in the history of American music, and a daring thing for Goodman to do.

Goodman hired Fletcher Henderson, also an African-American, to write arrangements for the band. Henderson's talent and ability helped the band become very popular.

Jazz writers and critics began to call Benny Goodman the "King of Swing." His theme song, "Let's Dance," was known by young people everywhere. In 1937, the band played the Paramount Theater in New York. Members of the audience jumped out of their seats and began to dance in the aisles. Outside, the crowd waiting to get in became uncontrollable.[12] The police had to be called to restore order.

Late that same year it was announced that Goodman would play a jazz concert in Carnegie Hall, the country's most famous concert hall. Carnegie Hall was home to opera, symphony orchestras, ballet, and performances by classical artists, but jazz had never been performed there.

Crowds often went wild when Goodman played his music.

The concert on January 16, 1938, was a tremendous success. The performers received several standing ovations. Jazz finally had been accepted as "real" music. Benny Goodman was famous, and he was not yet thirty years old.

After his triumph in Carnegie Hall, Goodman led his band in concerts and on tours. He also played with a number of classical music groups, including the New York, Cleveland, Pittsburgh, and National symphony orchestras. He often was a guest conductor and shared the stage with well-known classical artists. Some classical musicians resented a swing musician playing and directing their group. But Goodman could play as well as they did and easily held his own with them.

During World War II, many musicians joined the armed forces. Good players were hard to find. Goodman was unable to join any branch of the military because of back problems. Instead, he toured military bases, where he played for the men and women of the armed forces. During the war years, in 1942, Benny Goodman married Alice Duckworth, the sister of his friend John Hammond.

As the war was ending, the big band era, too, was ending. Another kind of jazz called bebop was becoming popular. Goodman did not like the new music and went into semiretirement. He still played with both jazz and classical groups, but he devoted most of his time to writing and arranging.

In 1955 *The Benny Goodman Story* was made in Hollywood. The information about his life was not very accurate, but people enjoyed the film. The music reminded them of the days when the swing bands were popular.

Although Benny was semiretired, his career was not over. He toured the Far East for the U.S. State Department, and in 1962 he and the band went to Russia (then known as the Soviet Union). It was the first time Russians had seen or heard a group of American jazz artists.[13] One of the songs he recorded as a result of the tour was called "Mission to Moscow."

In 1978, forty years after his first concert in Carnegie Hall, Goodman returned to play there again. By the end of the first day that tickets went on sale, the concert was sold out. The audience in 1978 was as enthusiastic about his music as the audience in 1938 had been.

Not too long after his second Carnegie Hall concert, Benny Goodman retired, but still not completely. He continued to play on rare occasions, usually as a soloist or with a small group. On June 13, 1986, Benny Goodman died of a heart attack.

Although Benny Goodman is gone, his music is still with us. His records have been preserved, and many are available on tape and compact disc. Films in which he appeared can be found in video stores everywhere. His personal record collection is at Harvard University's library.

Benny Goodman left the world a rich heritage of music. But perhaps his most important contributions were bringing jazz and classical music together and his early efforts at integrating white and African-American musicians. Benny Goodman had earned the title of the King of Swing.

6

John Birks Gillespie
"Dizzy"

Just about the time World War II ended, so did the era of swing music. Many musicians returning from World War II, and a lot of the youngsters who had replaced them while they were away, were interested in experimenting with music. They wanted a change from the highly structured music they played before the war. A new kind of jazz called bebop, or bop, was being created.

Bop was the music of the small group: trios, quartets, quintets. Unlike the swing music of the 1930s and 1940s, bop involved improvisation and a constant changing of chords, music that was difficult for large groups to play. Bop was music for listening, not dancing. And bop was played so rapidly and with

John Birks Gillespie

so many notes, it was difficult for listeners to follow the melody.[1]

To some musicians, bop was a way of protesting racial discrimination. African-American musicians wanted to be treated as equals—to be recognized as artists and to earn the same pay as white musicians.[2] For John Gillespie and others, however, bop was a technical innovation, not a political protest.

John Birks Gillespie, known to his fans as Dizzy, Diz, or Ole Diz, was born on October 21, 1917, in Cheraw, South Carolina. He grew up in the segregated South. It was a part of the country where people of color did not have the same freedoms or rights as white people.

In the South, African-American children were unable to go to the same schools as whites. They could not play in the same parks or on the same playgrounds as white people or even drink out of the same water fountains.

Young John Gillespie knew he was not allowed to live in the same neighborhoods or eat in the same restaurants as whites. And when he rode on trains or buses, he had to ride in a separate car or all the way in the back. He learned as a child that if he were approached by a white person while walking down the street, he would have to step off the curb and into the street.[3] John also learned that things were better for an African-American person in the North.

John was the ninth and last child of Lottie and James Gillespie. His father, who was a bricklayer, led an amateur band. By hanging around with his father and listening to the band, John was exposed to many different musical instruments.

When he was thirteen, he began to play the trombone. He took some lessons, but he mostly taught himself.[4] A year later he switched to trumpet because his arms were too short to play all the notes on the trombone.[5]

In high school he played trumpet in the band and participated in sports. He had enough musical talent to win a scholarship to Laurinburg Institute, a private African-American vocational school in North Carolina. There he also played trumpet, although the school didn't have anyone to teach him more about the instrument. During his two years at Laurinburg, he played a lot of music, which helped him sharpen his skills.

Just before his graduation from Laurinburg in 1935, his mother moved to Philadelphia. He joined her, leaving school before his graduation. Although his formal education ended then, he would return to Laurinburg thirteen years later to receive his high school diploma.[6]

In Philadelphia, Gillespie began to play with small groups. A short time later, he played in a big band, the Frank Fairfax Orchestra. It was while playing with Fairfax that he got the nickname Dizzy, because he was always clowning around and doing crazy things.[7] Dizzy's behavior never changed, and the nickname stuck. He has been called Dizzy, Diz, or Ole Diz ever since.

When he was twenty, he moved to New York. He joined Teddy Hill's orchestra,[8] but he wasn't popular with the other musicians. They said his antics disrupted the music.[9] Nevertheless, Dizzy later turned out to be a very good and stable musician.

In the fall of 1939, Dizzy joined Cab Calloway. It was while playing with Calloway that he became interested in blending jazz with Cuban and African rhythms and tones.[10] He also began writing musical arrangements for big bands. His music began to take on some of the elements of bebop.

Calloway didn't approve of Dizzy's onstage antics. He didn't like the way Dizzy played. He called his music "Chinese music."[11] Their disagreements became more frequent and tense. Finally, Calloway accused him of throwing spitballs during a concert. They had a brief fistfight and Calloway fired him.[12]

After he left Calloway, Dizzy played with Ella Fitzgerald, Charlie Barnett, Fletcher Henderson, Benny Carter, and Earl Hines, some of the great musicians of the time.[13] He had developed his own style and was working steadily, but he felt the people with whom he was playing were too traditional. He wanted to branch out and experiment.

When Dizzy returned to New York, he began playing and experimenting in jam sessions with Charlie "Bird" Parker and others. He and Parker made several records together. During this time, he also joined Earl "Fatha" Hines, whose orchestra included Parker and Billy Eckstine.

When Billy Eckstine left the Hines band, he invited Dizzy to join him as player and music director.[14] Parker had also joined Eckstine, and he and Diz were hardly ever apart. They recorded together and jointly led a combo (a small jazz band) in a small club in New York.[15]

In 1945 Diz had organized a big band as part of a touring stage show. People didn't like the band because they couldn't dance to its music.[16] He disbanded the big group. He and Charlie Parker organized a smaller band and went on tour in California. The audiences still did not like their music, and Parker was losing his battle against drug addiction. They split up. They performed together only a few more times before Parker's death some ten years later.[17]

Dizzy started a second big band about a year later. By this time, bop had caught on. The band was successful. It played a concert in Carnegie Hall, made some records, and appeared in movies. The band also successfully blended African and Latin rhythms and sounds with jazz.[18]

Dizzy was an accomplished composer and arranger. In 1940, he composed "Pickin' the Cabbage" and "Paradiddle." In 1942 he composed "A Night in Tunisia" and "Salt Peanuts," then "Woody 'n You" and "Bebop" in 1944.[19] All were big hits with Dizzy's fans.

As the decade of the 1940s was becoming history, big bands were being replaced by small groups. Dizzy reorganized his quintet and toured the United States and Europe, creating excitement among his fans.

In 1953, while at a birthday party for his wife, someone fell on Dizzy's horn.[20] The bell was bent upward, and Diz got angry, thinking it could not be played again.[21] To his surprise, when he played it, the sound seemed to reach his ears better.[22] From that time on, he had all his horns made with the bell pointing up. He apparently was the only jazz trumpeter to play such an instrument.[23]

Dizzy never slowed down. In 1954 he played the first Newport Jazz Festival, and in 1956 the U.S. State Department sent the band on tour to Africa, the Near East, Asia, and Eastern Europe.[24] Following that tour, Dizzy traveled throughout South America.

In 1959 Dizzy and Louis Armstrong performed together publicly for the first time. That same year, Cheraw, South Carolina, celebrated Dizzy Gillespie Day. Dizzy played before the first integrated audience in South Carolina since the end of the Civil War.[25]

Dizzy was always a strong supporter of civil rights. Even the horn-rimmed glasses, cigarette holder, goatee, and beret were part of his protest about the treatment of African Americans. He was so distressed over racial segregation in the country that he campaigned for president in 1964. Although he eventually withdrew from the race, he claimed he ran for president not to promote himself, but because "I

Gillespie's puffed cheeks, his trumpet with the bell bent upward, and his experimental musical style set him apart from the other jazz musicians of his time.

have been deeply concerned with drawing attention to the dire necessity of bringing together the peoples of the world in unity so that all wars may cease."[26]

During the 1970s and 1980s, Dizzy continued to arrange, compose, and play. He toured with his band and played at major jazz festivals. Presidents, governors, and mayors, as well as kings and princes, admired and honored Diz. He played at the White House. He received honorary doctorates from Rutgers University (1972) and the Chicago Conservatory of Music (1979). He was given the Paul Robeson Award from the Rutgers University Institute of Jazz Studies in 1972, and he received a symbolic Key to the City from various communities, including Annapolis, Maryland. In 1975 he was given a citation by the mayor of New York City. Throughout the forties, fifties, and sixties, in almost every music poll conducted by various jazz magazines, he was named "best." He was a featured soloist at almost every jazz festival in the country. The list of the honors and awards he received fills over two pages in his autobiography, which covers his career only up to 1979.[27]

In the late 1980s, Dizzy continued to tour, even though he was considered an "elder statesman" of jazz.[28] In 1992, to celebrate his seventy-fifth birthday, he played in a New York club for eight weeks with musicians of his choosing.[29] He was not as strong as he once was, but his tones sounded as good as ever. Diz was a happy man.

John Birks Gillespie died of cancer on January 6, 1993. Dizzy will be remembered for the influence he had on younger trumpet players and for his efforts in promoting civil rights. The image of the man in the horn-rimmed glasses wearing a beret and with cheeks inflated like a hamster who had eaten too much will live long in the memory of jazz fans.

Charles Christopher Parker, Jr.

"Bird"

Bop was born during the many nightly jam sessions at Minton's, a club in New York City's Harlem section. It was the place where the young jazz artists gathered every night after work and, in the same way some people jog to reduce tension, played together. It was a time when they could relax, listen to one another, and improvise. The sessions would last until the early hours of the morning.

Bop had many creators. Some were unknown, and some, like Dizzy Gillespie, were already famous. But most jazz listeners would agree that the unquestioned master of the "new" music was Charlie Parker, who was called Bird or Yardbird.[1]

Charles Christopher Parker, Jr., was born in Kansas City, Kansas, on August 29, 1920. He was

Charles Christopher Parker, Jr.

the only son of Addie and Charles Parker, Sr. There was an older half brother, John, who was his father's child from a previous relationship. When young Charles was seven, the family moved across the river to Kansas City, Missouri.

Charles Parker, Sr., was a vaudeville performer who became a chef on the railroad. His heavy drinking and long periods away from home broke up the marriage. When Charlie was eleven, his father left and took John with him. Charlie saw him again only a couple of times,[2] but he did return home for his funeral in 1937.[3]

To help pay the bills, Addie rented the upstairs floor of the house to Fannie Ruffin. Mrs. Ruffin and her six daughters and son moved into the upstairs of the Parker house.[4] Almost immediately Charlie became interested in Rebecca, one of the daughters.[5]

Addie Parker adored Charles. When he expressed a mild interest in playing the saxophone, Addie bought him one. There were two music schools in Kansas City, but African Americans were not permitted to attend either. What formal music education Charlie had, he got in the public schools and from playing in the high school band.[6] He learned mostly from watching and listening to others.

School records indicate that he repeated his freshman year of high school and spent a lot of time as a truant.[7] His mother always said he was a good student, but she may have been trying to protect him. Charlie himself said he had not done well in school, and years later when asked about school he would say he "spent three years in high school and wound up a freshman."[8] At fifteen he dropped out.

His remaining teenage years were busy ones, however. On July 26, 1936, at the young age of sixteen, Charlie married Rebecca Ruffin, his childhood sweetheart.

Charlie was hanging around the clubs, playing when he was asked and listening to riff, a new jazz style that came from Africa and was developing in Kansas City.[9] Unfortunately, some of the musicians, no one knows whom, introduced Charlie to drugs.

Evidently Charlie was not well accepted by other musicians. He was unconventional and did not play like they did. They did not seem to understand his music. At one jam session when he tried to improvise, everyone laughed. He walked out and went home and cried.[10] Another time, when he was invited to play with Count Basie, the drummer threw a cymbal at his feet because he was playing off key and in the wrong time.[11]

Lawrence Keyes, a friend and neighbor who led a band called the Deans of Swing,[12] helped Charlie polish his playing and later took him into his band.

Charlie and Rebecca were not getting along. Charlie had an eye for women and was beginning to roam. When Rebecca became pregnant and was awaiting the birth of their child, Charlie started seeing another woman. On January 10, 1938, Charlie and Rebecca's son, Francis Leon, was born.[13]

Charlie drifted and roamed, playing with different groups around the area. He was bored with the music he was playing and wanted to try other ways. He said he could hear the music he wanted to play, but he couldn't play it.[14] He joined a band led by Jay McShann. The band played mostly riff and blues,[15] but Charlie quit after only three weeks. He couldn't seem to settle down, but then, he was only seventeen.

Charlie decided to go to New York, which was the center of jazz at the time. When he arrived, he learned that he couldn't play in the clubs there because he didn't belong to the musicians union. He worked as a dishwasher until he got his union card, then rejoined the McShann band.

Charlie felt restricted with the routines and arrangements of a big band. He wanted to try new techniques, but he was expected to play the music as it was written. When the band went to Detroit, Parker remained in New York.[16] But jobs were not easy to find, and he spent much time playing just for food and cigarette money. He also started spending a lot of time playing at Minton's in Harlem. The musicians who gathered at Minton's recognized Bird's abilities and skill and accepted him and his music without question.

Parker spent most of 1943 playing tenor sax with Earl Hines. Dizzy Gillespie was also in the band, and he and Bird became close friends. In April 1943 Parker married Geraldine Scott.[17]

71

Parker joined Billy Eckstine's band in 1944 but still could not adjust to playing in a big band. He and Dizzy quit Eckstine's band and headed for California. They played for a while at a Hollywood club, but Diz returned to New York. Parker remained in California and formed his own group, which featured Miles Davis.

During his stay in California, his dependency on drugs and alcohol increased. To make matters worse, the critics and most of the public did not like his music. Parker was under a lot of pressure. He returned to his hotel one night and set fire to his room. He suffered a mental and emotional breakdown and was committed to a mental hospital.

After six months, Parker was released from the hospital and returned to New York. To the public, he seemed to be a different person. He was energetic and he played well. He composed music and played steadily in New York for the next two years. He seemed to settle down. He and Geraldine divorced, and Doris Sydnor became his third wife.

Privately, however, Parker really wasn't much different. He was still using narcotics and drinking heavily. His health was very poor. And he still had the desire to roam.

In 1949 he made his first tour overseas, playing in Paris at the International Jazz Festival. When he returned, he was honored by the opening of a New York club that was named for him. It was called Birdland.

Parker did not like playing music note for note but, instead, loved to improvise. Although this sometimes got him in trouble with other musicians, it was also the reason he was considered a master of bop and had the jazz club Birdland named after him.

In mid-1950, Bird left his wife and moved in with Chan Richardson. Two children resulted from this union: a daughter, Pree; and a son, Charles Baird Parker.

Parker still had the wanderlust. He toured Sweden for a week in 1951. Then, he went to London. He was moving at a rapid pace and his health was worsening. Shortly after he returned from Europe, he suffered an attack of peptic ulcers.[18] But he kept going.

He played in Los Angeles again and in San Francisco, where he was fired and stranded for a week.[19] He returned to New York, but he was physically ill and mentally depressed.

His depression worsened in 1953 when Pree died of pneumonia. Parker attempted suicide. It apparently was not a serious attempt and he recovered. But the episode led to further problems with Chan. Finally they separated.

Parker was booked to play Birdland, but his behavior became very strange. When on the bandstand, he would play a tune different from what the band was playing. The club that was named in his honor could no longer tolerate his behavior, and it fired him.

Parker attempted suicide again and was sent to Bellevue Hospital. He was discharged but returned voluntarily eight days later. Released again, he played in a Town Hall concert the next month.

Parker returned to play at Birdland in March 1955. He fought on the bandstand with one of the musicians.[20] He was scheduled to play in Boston a few days later. Before he left, however, he dropped by the Stanhope Hotel to see a wealthy jazz fan who was a friend of his. He became ill while visiting and a doctor was called.

He was desperately ill and he knew it. He called his mother, who wanted him to come home to Kansas City. He didn't go anywhere, however, not even to a hospital. He died at the hotel on March 12, 1955, from pneumonia brought on by his hard lifestyle.

The tragedy of Charlie Parker is that what might have been a long and productive life was cut short by a negative lifestyle. Yet Charlie Parker was a jazz giant. His break from the structure of the big band music gave rise to bebop. His boldness in playing music as he felt it and his individualism gave courage to hundreds of young musicians to experiment and innovate with their music. Although he was a saxophonist, jazz instrumentalists of all kinds copy his style. Sadly, it was only after his death that he achieved the recognition and acceptance he craved during his lifetime.

Miles Dewey Davis, III

Miles Dewey Davis, III

"The Phoenix of Jazz"

In the myths of ancient Greece, the phoenix, a colorful bird, lived for five hundred years. It exploded in flames and then rose from its own ashes to live once again. Miles Davis, of course, didn't live that many years, but each time people thought he had burned out, like the phoenix he rose again and returned to the top of the jazz world.

Miles Dewey Davis, III, was born on May 25, 1926, in Alton, Illinois. He came from a wealthy and well-educated family. His father, a dentist, was a proud man who believed strongly in the rights of African Americans.

When Davis was a year old, the family moved to East St. Louis, just across the Mississippi River from St. Louis, Missouri. In East St. Louis, the family lived in a middle-class white neighborhood. Miles grew up with both African-American and white friends. He said his pride in being African-American came from his father.[1]

East St. Louis had been the scene of a race riot in 1917. Although nothing had happened since, African-American citizens were expected to "stay in their place." Miles and his brother and sister attended an all-African-American elementary school, where they had very good teachers,[2] but the poor conditions of the building left Miles with bitter memories.[3] He also experienced other racial incidents both in and out of school,[4] including being called racial names.[5] It's not surprising that Miles became a moody and withdrawn person.

Also contributing to his gloomy personality was his life at home. Miles didn't get along well with his mother.[6] Apparently his father didn't either. He and Mrs. Davis argued and fought. Life in the Davis household apparently was not quiet or smooth. In his autobiography, Miles describes some of the arguments that occurred in the house.[7]

As a young boy, Miles was interested in sports. He was a good athlete, although a bit too skinny to be a star. When he was given an old trumpet by a friend of his father's,[8] he started to take music lessons. By the time he was twelve, music was his only interest. His father realized how serious young Miles was about music, so for his thirteenth birthday he bought him a new trumpet.

His father and mother wanted Miles to learn classical music because they disapproved of the popular music of the day. But the boy was listening secretly to the music of Jimmie Lunceford, Louis Armstrong, Duke Ellington, Bessie Smith, and others. He was hooked on jazz.[9]

For a youngster dazzled by jazz, St. Louis was a good place to be. There were a number of excellent musicians from the area, and many of the bands from New York, New Orleans, and Kansas City came to St. Louis to play.[10]

When he was seventeen, he landed his first real job playing in a band, the Blue Devils. While playing in this band he met Clark Terry, a trumpeter from St. Louis. Terry, who became a lifelong friend, introduced Miles to various musicians and took him to jam sessions around the area.

He also met Charlie "Bird" Parker and Dizzy Gillespie when they passed through town while playing with Billy Eckstine's band.[11] In the spring of 1944, Dizzy Gillespie, who had heard Miles play, asked Miles to join his group for two weeks to replace a sick trumpet player.

After high school in 1944, Davis left for New York to study at Juilliard, one of the nation's most outstanding schools of music. He was supposed to study classical music and composing, which he did during the daytime. But at night Davis traveled from club to club, listening to jazz. He was particularly impressed by Charlie Parker and his music. On occasion he played in Parker's quintet when Dizzy Gillespie wasn't available.[12]

In the autumn of 1945, when Dizzy Gillespie left the Parker quintet, Parker asked Miles to join the group. Miles agreed and returned home to tell his father he had quit Juilliard. He was pleased and surprised when his father encouraged him to do his best.[13]

Davis played mostly with Parker until 1948, when he formed his own band. The band was a flop.[14] However, it was one of the first groups to record "cool jazz." Unlike the explosive bebop, cool was a softer, more structured type of jazz. It was a kind of jazz that used some techniques and instruments, French horns, for example, from classical music.[15] The band's recording of "The Birth of the Cool" has become a classic. It marked the birth of a new phase of jazz.

Davis played at the Paris Jazz Festival in 1949 and became well known in Europe. Then his career seemed to come to a complete halt. He worked with various groups and individuals, but he seemed to have lost his direction and drive. There was a reason. Davis had become addicted to heroin.

Many people tried to help him. His father took him back to Illinois for a while. But nothing worked. Davis couldn't break his habit. He returned to New York, made some records, and played occasionally with Bird and Dizzy, but he simply wasn't himself.

The jazz scene was moving west, and it became harder and harder for Davis to get work in New York. Bored with life, he left for California. But life in California wasn't any better, so he returned to Illinois once again.

In a desperate move to kick his heroin habit, Davis locked himself in a small house on his father's farm. For about seven or eight days, he suffered the pains of withdrawal.[16] But he broke his habit. It was 1954 and time to put his life back together.

In 1955 Davis performed at the Newport Jazz Festival and drove the crowd into a frenzy.[17] Like the phoenix, Miles Davis had risen again.

During the latter half of the 1950s, Davis became the major figure in jazz. His first quintet was organized in 1955, and in 1959 his sextet recorded *Kind of Blue*, which is considered by many to be the most influential recording in jazz history.[18] Adding a sixth instrument gave Davis more of an opportunity to create different sounds.

The 1960s was the decade of rock music, and Davis became concerned that young African Americans would lose touch with jazz. He considered jazz a part of the culture of African Americans, so he began experimenting by blending the two. It worked, and fusion, another form of jazz, was born.[19] One more time, Miles had contributed to a new form of jazz.

Davis was always trying new approaches to his music. He introduced electric instruments into his music, one of the first jazz musicians to do so. He also used African and Indian instruments and rhythms in his work.

Miles retired in the 1970s. Health problems and injuries from an auto accident, combined with his frantic pace, began to wear him down. And he was again using drugs, this time cocaine.

He said that from 1975 to early 1980 he did not pick up his horn.[20] But in 1981 he made a long-awaited comeback at the New York Jazz Festival.[21] The "phoenix" had risen again, and there was little argument about his greatness.

Miles Davis was always a controversial person. He sometimes played with his back to the crowd.[22] He said he did what he wanted to do and offered no explanations or apologies. Nor did he try to hide his dislike of many white people.[23]

Davis always looked ahead. He never talked about the past, nor did he continue to play his old songs.[24] He surprised his friends in 1989 when he published his autobiography and in 1991 when he played all of his old songs at a concert in France.

During his professional career, Miles Davis toured most of the globe and had many honors and awards bestowed upon him. He received the *Esquire* magazine New Star Award for Trumpet (1947) and the Sonning Music Award for Lifetime Achievement (1984), an award usually given to classical musicians. He twice tied Dizzy Gillespie for the *Down Beat* magazine jazz award (1947 and 1955) and was

Miles Dewey Davis, III

Always on the cutting edge, Davis contributed to the development
of cool, modal, and fusion jazz.

named to the Metronome All-Stars in 1949. He was
honored at Radio City Music Hall in New York in
1983 at a celebration called "Miles Ahead: A Tribute
to an American Music Legend."[25] Also in 1983 Davis
was awarded an honorary degree from Fisk
University, the institution his mother had wanted
him to attend.[26] Miles Davis had become a giant in
the world of jazz.

Davis was known and admired all over the world.
Other musicians copied his style, his mannerisms,
and his manner of dress. No other individual was as
closely involved in the development of three major
phases of jazz—cool, modal, and fusion—as he.

As the last decade of the twentieth century began,
illness and exhaustion began to take its toll. Davis's
strength was practically gone. But he still played and
was active to the end. On September 29, 1991, Miles
Davis died from complications of pneumonia, respi-
ratory failure, and a stroke, brought about, in part at
least, by his hard lifestyle. He was sixty-five years old.

The phoenix would rise no more.

John Coltrane

"Trane"

Jazz lovers remember John Coltrane for his artistic ability. Musicians praised him as a devoted teacher who was always willing to help young artists develop their careers. His admirers claim that his outlook on life and his music influenced everyone around him. Even today, many music critics claim "Trane" was one of most influential figures in modern jazz.

Born in Hamlet, North Carolina, on September 23, 1926, John Coltrane grew up in High Point, about one hundred miles away. He and his mother and father lived with Mrs. Coltrane's parents, the Reverend and Mrs. Blair. It was a devoutly religious and churchgoing household. John's religious background would influence his entire adult life and his

John Coltrane

music. In his adult years, his music would focus on his religious beliefs.

John Coltrane grew up with music. No one in the family was a professional musician, but his father, a tailor, was a self-taught violin player. He loved country music and entertained the young John with some of his songs. His mother played piano and sang in church. She believed that music should be a part of John's education.

When John was thirteen, he joined a church band. He wanted to play the clarinet but was given an alto saxophone.[1] When one of the clarinet players didn't come to practice, John took the clarinet and played a few notes. The band director, who liked only marches and church music, was so impressed with John's tone, he switched him to the clarinet. He never knew that John had been listening secretly to jazz music.[2]

In school John was not an outstanding student in any subject except for music. He was so serious about the clarinet, he even practiced in the backyard. He practiced at all hours. Finally, the neighbors complained.[3] John moved his practicing indoors.

John played clarinet in the high school band, but he switched to alto saxophone when he was a senior. When he graduated in 1944, he moved to Philadelphia, where his mother had moved a few years before. He wanted to study music performance and composition so that he could be a musician.

Instead he joined the Navy and was assigned to play clarinet in a Navy band.

When he was discharged in 1946, he returned to Philadelphia. He intended to return to school but he had no money, so he joined a rhythm and blues band playing alto saxophone. Rhythm and blues, or R&B, became very popular in the late forties and early fifties. It was played mostly by African-American musicians and had practically replaced the swing music played by the big bands during the thirties and forties.

John had no trouble finding jobs. He played with several groups around Philadelphia. When he heard that one of the groups needed a tenor sax player, he switched from alto to tenor and got the job. Although he would learn to play several different instruments, the tenor saxophone would be his chief instrument.

John loved bebop, or bop. It may have been because it was very complex and challenging, or it may have been because his idol, Charlie "Bird" Parker, was deeply into it. Those who knew him say it also was because bop was a form of social protest for young African-American men over the treatment of their people.[4] Whatever the reasons, John joined Dizzy Gillespie, the big man in bop, in 1948. He remained with him until 1951. After he left Gillespie, Coltrane returned to Philadelphia. He played in a few different groups and began to study music. It was around this time he began to use heroin.[5] He also started drinking. He said he suffered from bad teeth and was in pain while he played. In order to dull the pain and get some sleep, he would drink.[6]

The drinking and drug abuse got worse. He still played but would disappear for long periods. He was overweight and sometimes fell asleep on the bandstand. Coltrane struggled to survive as an individual and as a musician.

In 1955 he joined the Miles Davis quintet. While with Davis he recorded "Round about Midnight." His solo on the record made him known throughout the jazz world.[7]

Early in 1957, with the help of Naima, his wife of two years, and his mother, Coltrane kicked both his drug habit and his addiction to alcohol.[8] He said he experienced a spiritual awakening. Always a devout person, he became even more religious.

Coltrane was now very intense about his music. LeRoi Jones (Amiri Baraka), an African-American playwright and friend, said, "Music for Trane was a way into God."[9] Trane moved away from bop and searched for new techniques and sounds. He read about music and musical theory. He practiced hour after hour. Sometimes he played so long and hard, he would collapse. Nothing seemed to matter except his music. His friend and fellow saxophonist, Julian "Cannonball" Adderley, said, "Sometimes he even fell asleep with the horn in his mouth."[10] Trane started to move away from bop and searched for new techniques and sounds.

He joined Miles Davis again, and together they made many records. Their styles blended well and their music was very popular. He explored other musical forms. And he practiced. He never seemed to be satisfied with his playing. He was like a man on a mission.[11]

In October 1960, Trane formed his own quartet. He also took time to master the soprano saxophone with its haunting tone. He continued to experiment with different and unusual sounds.

Early in the 1960s, he developed an interest in the musical sounds and rhythms of Africa and India. He became one of the first musicians to blend the instruments and music of the East into his own music.[12] He admired the music of India. He was so impressed with Ravi Shankar, the great Indian sitar (a guitar-like instrument) player, that he named his second son Ravi.[13]

Trane was passionate about everything he did. He was known for long solos. He once told Miles Davis that when he started a solo, he didn't know how to stop. Davis is supposed to have said, "Try taking the saxophone out of your mouth."[14] And one critic said, "He often plays his tenor sax as if he were determined to blow it apart."[15]

Trane's music reflected his feelings about the Watts riot and the Selma-to-Montgomery civil rights march. "Alabama," one of the songs on his album

By the early 1960s, Coltrane had mastered the soprano saxophone.

Coltrane Live at Birdland, was inspired by one of Martin Luther King, Jr.'s speeches about the bombing of an African-American church.[16] Other music revealed his feelings about other events during the unrest and strife of the 1960s. Most notable, perhaps, is "Kulu Sé Mama." It is a blending of African drum rhythms and free jazz.[17]

Trane made several successful tours of Europe. The fans in the countries he visited were just as fond of his music as the fans in America. Most other musicians would have been pleased and satisfied with that kind of success. Not Trane. He continued to experiment with music and sounds of all kinds. He needed to do better.

He developed an intense interest in free jazz, a form of jazz music with no limits or rules. But free jazz failed to win support from listeners. Some thought it was the jazz artists' way of rebelling against bop.

Many fans were disappointed and displeased at the direction his music was taking. But others still adored him. Trane had suffered criticism before, so he continued to work hard and search for the "right sound."

By 1965 Trane had stopped playing typical modern jazz. His playing became very emotional. He believed that music was a form of meditation or prayer. His religious beliefs were reflected in the titles of many of his recordings, such as *A Love Supreme,*

Ascension, The Father and the Son, and *The Holy Ghost.*

In 1966, John Coltrane was at the peak of his career. He had made an immensely successful tour of Japan. He was wealthy. He was named top jazz artist in many polls. He owned a beautiful house outside New York City. He had recording contracts and even owned his own publishing company. Yet he wasn't completely happy. He was still searching for that perfect sound.

In 1966 Trane's health began to fail. He suffered constantly from fatigue, even though he followed a rigid diet. He became very concerned about his health and well-being. In May, while he was visiting his mother, he became very ill. He returned to New York City and on July 16 was hospitalized. The years of heavy drinking and substance abuse had done their damage. It was too late. The next day Trane died of liver cancer. He was not quite forty-one years old.

During his short and emotionally torn lifetime, John Coltrane changed forever the way jazz is played. Musicians still copy his style, and jazz writers and critics still remember him fondly. John Coltrane was a quiet boy from a quiet little town in North Carolina, but in the world of jazz he was a titan.

Wynton Marsalis

"Back to the Future"

When we hear the word *revolution*, most of us think of a brave person leading an army into battle or saving someone's life. That's usually the way it is in the movies and on television. But *revolution* also means "change." Today, many people believe Wynton Marsalis has revolutionized the world of jazz.

Wynton was born in New Orleans on October 18, 1961, the son of Ellis and Dolores Marsalis. He was born into a musical family. Three of his five brothers are excellent musicians.[1] Delfeayo plays trombone. Jason is a drummer. Branford, an accomplished saxophonist, is almost as well known as Wynton.

Wynton Marsalis

The father of the group, Ellis, is a jazz pianist, composer, and teacher. He was active in bebop in the 1960s. Although she was not a musician, Dolores Marsalis had a deep appreciation for music. She supported the efforts of her boys. And it was she, through her strong Roman Catholic upbringing and high standards, who taught the boys a sense of order and the self-discipline necessary to become successful.[2]

Wynton got his first trumpet when he was six. Al Hirt, a famous jazz player and friend of his father, gave it to him.[3] Wynton's first teacher was his father. Wynton took to the trumpet easily and learned quickly. After just two years he was playing in a children's marching band.[4]

When Wynton was twelve he became a student at the New Orleans Center for Creative Arts. It was a perfect match. At the center he studied Bach and Beethoven, but he could also pursue his interest in jazz.[5] His jazz playing was strongly influenced by the music of Charlie Parker and John Coltrane. He listened to the music of many great trumpeters. His style was greatly influenced by Louis Armstrong, Fats Navarro, and Clifford Brown.[6]

At age fourteen he won a local contest playing Haydn's Concert in E–flat Major for Trumpet and Orchestra. It is a piece of music that is difficult for even an adult to play. As the winner, Wynton was given the opportunity to play the concerto with the New Orleans Philharmonic Orchestra.[7]

Two years later, at age sixteen, Wynton won the same competition again. People began to realize that Wynton was probably a musical genius.

The young Marsalis seemed to adapt easily to any type of music. He could play jazz and he could play classical music. While playing in his high school band, he was also playing first trumpet in the New Orleans Civic Orchestra.[8] The first trumpet in any symphony orchestra is usually an experienced player. Such a position is rarely given to a teenage musician. But Wynton was not a typical teenage musician.

In 1978, when he was seventeen, Wynton attended the Berkshire Music Center at Tanglewood,[9] one of the country's most prestigious summer schools for young musicians. At Tanglewood his playing and knowledge of music got the attention of Gunter Schuller, a musician, writer, composer, and music critic[10] known for his ability to play both classical music and jazz.[11] He thought Wynton was an excellent player. The teachers at Tanglewood apparently agreed. They presented Wynton with the award as the outstanding brass player of the summer.[12]

At age eighteen, Wynton left New Orleans for New York, where he enrolled at the famous Juilliard School.[13] He intended to follow a career playing classical music.[14] After a short time at Juilliard, he left. He had joined Art Blakey's Jazz Messengers, one of the outstanding musical groups at that time. Playing with Blakey gave him experience and allowed him to display his talents to many people.

In 1981 he joined Herbie Hancock's jazz quartet. They played at the Newport Jazz Festival and then in New York. The group also toured Japan.[15] The tour helped Marsalis establish a reputation as an exceptional musician.[16]

While he was playing with Hancock, Wynton recorded his first album. It was named, appropriately, *Wynton Marsalis*. The album received excellent reviews.

The next year, Marsalis formed his own quintet. It included his brother Branford. They played a concert with the Kool All-Stars. They also played a benefit concert for Thelonious Monk, a well-known jazz pianist and composer.

Wynton took his quintet on a long tour of Europe. The jazz fans there loved his music. Following that tour, the group played in Japan. Then, Wynton returned to England, where he recorded his first classical album.

While in London, Marsalis met Maurice Andre, perhaps the most famous classical trumpet player in the world. Andre said Marsalis was "potentially the greatest classical trumpeter of all time."[17]

In 1983, when Marsalis was twenty-two, the band went on tour again. It played in Europe and the Far East. In addition to playing with the band, Marsalis conducted workshops and seminars on jazz. He lectured and played at various music festivals.

Marsalis plays all music with the same deep feeling and enthusiasm. He is the first musician who has been completely accepted by artists in both the classical and jazz worlds.[18]

In the summer of 1984, Marsalis made a classical music tour of the United States and Canada. He also performed that summer in London. During that year, also, he made an important career decision. He decided he could not achieve excellence in both jazz and classical music. He chose jazz. And because he believed jazz required more skill than classical music, he quit performing at concerts that featured classical music.

In 1984, the year Marsalis made his decision, he became the first musician to win a Grammy award for Best Jazz Soloist and another for Best Classical Music Soloist with Orchestra.[19] Since making his decision, Marsalis has performed classical music only when recording in a studio.[20]

Marsalis began to study jazz. He started at the present and worked backward to the early days of New Orleans jazz.[21] He investigated its early roots. He studied the blues, gospel music, and work songs. He spent considerable time learning all he could about Louis Armstrong and Duke Ellington and their music.[22]

Miles Davis, who was one of Marsalis's models, believed that there was no absolute definition of jazz. He argued that jazz could evolve into many different kinds of music. Marsalis, on the other hand, believes in a narrow definition of jazz.[23] He argues for "a return to jazz purity."[24] Most jazz authorities believe

Although Marsalis was also a great classical trumpeter, he decided to focus on jazz because he believed it required more skill.

that Marsalis represents a return to what might be called conservative values in music. His views have created much debate and discussion in the music business.

During the 1990s, Marsalis has maintained a busy schedule. He has given concerts. He has made recordings. He has spoken about music to school-children all over the country. He has acted as performer and narrator on television programs aimed at young people. *Marsalis on Music* is one example of his work. It is a series of four television productions explaining and demonstrating the resemblances and differences between jazz and European classical music.[25]

In April 1992, the Lincoln Center for the Performing Arts created a permanent department of jazz. Wynton Marsalis was its first artistic director.[26] As director, Marsalis highlighted the music of the old masters: "Jelly Roll" Morton, Duke Ellington, and Louis Armstrong.[27] This, of course, reflected his belief that the future of jazz can be found, in large part, in its past. It also created controversy.

The focus on the "old-timers" and his omission of tributes to white musicians resulted in charges that Marsalis was racist. To complicate matters, he attempted to fire all musicians over the age of thirty. This blunder brought about charges of age discrimination.[28] His first year as director was neither quiet nor uneventful.

In 1993 he made an international tour with his seven-man group.[29] He played concerts and conducted workshops on jazz.

Marsalis has written two books. In 1994 *Sweet Swing Blues on the Road* was published, and the following year, *Marsalis on Music.* Both books received positive reviews, demonstrating that Marsalis can both write and play the trumpet well. In April 1997, Marsalis won the 1997 Pulitzer Prize in music for his composition *Blood on the Fields.*

At thirty-five years of age, most individuals are still trying to climb the ladder of success. They are struggling to establish an identity in their chosen field. At an age when most musicians are still trying to perfect techniques and style, Wynton Marsalis is a superstar. There is little debate regarding his ability to play. He is recognized as one of the best trumpeters in the world. When asked to judge the ability of a particular musician, Leonard Feather, a noted jazz critic, said, "He's the Wynton Marsalis of the clarinet."[30] Now that's some compliment!

Wynton Marsalis continues to amaze the world with his talent. His schedule still includes playing, teaching, and writing. He is firm in his belief that the future of jazz can be found in its past. He may be right. Only time will tell.

Chapter Notes

Chapter 1. Scott Joplin: "King of Ragtime"

1. James M. Smallwood, *Time of Hope, Time of Despair: Black Texans During Reconstruction,* cited in Susan Curtis, *Dancing to a Black Man's Tune: A Life of Scott Joplin* (Columbia: University of Missouri Press, 1994), p. 29.

2. Curtis, p. 19.

3. Peter Gammond, *Scott Joplin and the Ragtime Era* (New York: St. Martin's Press, 1975), p. 28

4. James Haskins with Kathleen Benson, *Scott Joplin* (Garden City, N.Y.: Doubleday & Company, Inc., 1978), p. 32.

5. Gammond, p. 28.

6. Haskins, p. 48.

7. Curtis, p. 36.

8. Gammond, p. 28.

9. Curtis, p. 36.

10. Gammond, p. 29.

11. Curtis, p. 38.

12. Gammond, p. 45.

13. Curtis, p. 48.

14. Ibid., p. 55.

15. Gammond, p. 46.

16. Curtis, p. 55

17. Gammond, p. 58.

18. Ibid., p. 60.

19. Haskins, p. 92.

20. Gammond, p. 62.

21. John Fordham, *Jazz* (New York: Dorling Kindersley, 1993), p. 126.

22. Grover Sales, *Jazz: America's Classical Music* (New York: Da Capo Press, Inc., 1992), p. 51.

23. Joachim Berendt, *The Jazz Book: From Ragtime to Fusion and Beyond,* sixth edition, revised by Gunther Huesmann (Brooklyn, N.Y.: Lawrence Hill Books, 1991), p. 8.

24. Gammond, p. 63.

25. Curtis, p. 70; Haskins, p. 100.

26. Gammond, p. 64.

27. Curtis, p. 94.

28. Ibid., p. 153.

29. Ibid., p. 159.

30. Haskins, p. 190.

Chapter 2. Daniel Louis Armstrong: "Satchmo"

1. Barry Kernfield, ed., *New Grove Dictionary of Jazz,* vol. 1 (London: Macmillan Press, Ltd., 1988), p. 27.

2. Leonard Feather, *The Encyclopedia of Jazz* (New York: Da Capo Press, 1960), p. 103.

3. Joachim Berendt, *The Jazz Book: From Ragtime to Fusion and Beyond,* sixth edition, revised by Gunther Huesmann (Brooklyn, N.Y.: Lawrence Hill Books, 1991), p. 64.

4. Kernfield, p. 27.

5. Davis Gates, "Louis Will Never Go Away," *Newsweek,* July 7, 1997, p. 66.

6. John Fordham, *Jazz* (New York: Dorling Kindersley, 1993), p. 96.

7. Len Lyons and Don Perlo, *Jazz Portraits* (New York: William Morrow, Inc., 1989), p. 34; Grover Sales, *Jazz: America's Classical Music* (New York: Da Capo Press, Inc., 1992), p. 59.

8. Fordham, p. 97.

9. Kernfield, p. 103.

10. Feather, p. 103.
11. Leo Walker, *The Big Band Almanac,* revised edition (New York: Da Capo Press, Inc., 1978), p. 11.
12. Ibid.
13. Ibid.

Chapter 3. Edward Kennedy Ellington: "Duke"
1. John E. Hasse, *Beyond Category: The Life and Genius of Duke Ellington* (New York: Simon & Schuster, 1993), p. 13.
2. Ken Rattenbury, *Duke Ellington: Jazz Composer* (New Haven: Yale University Press, 1990), p. 280.
3. Hasse, p. 21.
4. Duke Ellington, *Music Is My Mistress* (Garden City, N.Y.: Doubleday & Company, Inc., 1973), p. 17.
5. Rattenbury, p. 280.
6. James L. Collier, *Duke Ellington,* (New York: Oxford University Press), p. 19.
7. Mark Tucker, *Ellington: The Early Years* (Urbana: University of Illinois Press, 1991), p. 8.
8. Hasse, p. 38; Mark Tucker, *The Duke Ellington Reader* (New York: Oxford University Press, 1993), p. 12.
9. Derek Jewell, *Duke: A Portrait of Duke Ellington* (New York: W. W. Norton, 1977), p. 27.
10. Ibid., p. 28.
11. Leonard Feather, *From Satchmo to Miles* (New York: Stein and Day, 1972), p. 50.
12. Hasse, p. 43.
13. Feather, p. 51.
14. Hasse, p. 133.
15. Jewell, p. 48.
16. Barry Kernfield, ed., *New Grove Dictionary of Jazz,* vol. 1 (London: Macmillan Press, Ltd., 1988), p. 332.

17. Carr, p. 190.

18. Joachim Berendt, *The Jazz Book: From Ragtime to Fusion and Beyond,* sixth edition, revised by Gunther Huesmann (Brooklyn, N.Y.: Lawrence Hill Books, 1991), p. 78.

19. Tucker, *The Duke Ellington Reader,* pp. 290–292.

20. Feather, p. 53.

21. Hasse, pp. 339, 340.

22. Ibid., p. 340.

23. Ibid., p. 358.

24. Feather, p. 54.

25. Ibid., p. 55.

26. Kernfield, p. 331.

27. Ibid., p. 331.

Chapter 4. Mary Lou Williams: "First Lady of Jazz"

1. Leslie Gourse, *Madame Jazz* (New York: Oxford University Press, 1995), p. 8.

2. Robert Gottlieb, ed., *Reading Jazz* (New York: Pantheon, 1996), p. 87.

3. Burton W. Peretti, *The Creation of Jazz* (Urbana: University of Illinois Press, 1994), p. 105.

4. Len Lyons, *The Great Jazz Pianists* (New York: Da Capo Press, Inc., 1983), p. 70.

5. Gottlieb, p. 87.

6. Ibid., p. 88.

7. Ibid.

8. Peretti, p. 122.

9. Gottlieb, p. 89.

10. Ibid., p. 90.

11. Ibid., p. 91.

12. Barry Kernfield, ed., *New Grove Dictionary of Jazz,* vol. 1 (London: Macmillan Press, Ltd., 1988), p. 626.

13. Kernfield, p. 627.
14. Gottlieb, p. 101.
15. Gottlieb, p. 106.
16. Gottlieb, p. 107.
17. Kernfield, p. 627.
18. Gottlieb, p. 110.
19. Kernfield, p. 627.
20. Grover Sales, *Jazz: America's Classical Music* (New York: Da Capo Press, Inc., 1992), p. 131.
21. Kernfield, p. 627.
22. Ibid.
23. Marian McPartland, *All in Good Time* (New York: Oxford University Press, 1987), p. 73.
24. Lyons, p. 69.
25. Ian Carr, Digby Fairweather, and Brian Priestley, *Jazz: The Rough Guide* (London: Rough Guides, Ltd., 1995), p. 698.
26. Lyons, p. 69.
27. Kernfield, p. 627.
28. Lyons, p. 69.
29. McPartland, p. 69.
30. Lyons, p. 68.

Chapter 5. Benjamin David Goodman: "The King of Swing"
1. Barry Kernfield, ed., *New Grove Dictionary of Jazz*, vol. 1 (London: Macmillan Press, Ltd., 1988), p. 438.
2. Len Lyons and Don Perlo, *Jazz Portraits* (New York: William Morrow, Inc., 1989), p. 227.
3. Grover Sales, *Jazz: America's Classical Music* (New York: Da Capo Press, Inc., 1992), p. 106.
4. Burton W. Peretti, *The Creation of Jazz* (Urbana: University of Illinois Press, 1994), p. 134.
5. Ibid., pp. 82, 83.

6. Bruce Crowther and Mike Pinfold, *The Big Band Years* (New York: Facts on File, 1988), p. 71.

7. George T. Simon, *The Big Bands* (New York: The Macmillan Company, 1965), p. 206.

8. Leo Walker, *The Big Band Almanac* (New York: Da Capo Press, 1989), p. 149.

9. Sales, p. 26.

10. Ibid., p. 28.

11. Ibid., p. 111.

12. Ian Carr, Digby Fairweather, and Brian Priestley, *Jazz: The Rough Guide* (London: Rough Guides, Ltd., 1995), p. 244.

13. Simon, p. 22.

Chapter 6. John Birks Gillespie: "Dizzy"

1. Eileen Southern, *The Music of Black Americans* (New York: W. W. Norton, 1997), p. 492.

2. Grover Sales, *Jazz: America's Classical Music* (New York: Da Capo Press, Inc., 1992), p. 131.

3. Sales, p. 111.

4. Ian Carr, Digby Fairweather, and Brian Priestley, *Jazz: The Rough Guide* (London: Rough Guides, Ltd., 1995), p. 234.

5. Len Lyons and Don Perlo, *Jazz Portraits* (New York: William Morrow, Inc., 1989), p. 218.

6. Dizzy Gillespie (with Al Fraser), *To Be, or Not . . . To Bop* (Garden City, N.Y.: Doubleday & Company, Inc., 1979), p. 347.

7. Barry Kernfield, ed., *New Grove Dictionary of Jazz,* vol. 1 (London: Macmillan Press, Ltd., 1988), p. 428.

8. Joachim Berendt, *The Jazz Book: From Ragtime to Fusion and Beyond,* sixth edition, revised by Gunther

Huesmann (Brooklyn, N.Y.: Lawrence Hill Books, 1991), p. 90.

9. Leonard Feather, *The Encyclopedia of Jazz* (New York: Da Capo Press, 1960), p. 226.

10. Carr, Fairweather, and Priestly, p. 235.

11. Lyons and Perlo, p. 220.

12. Ibid.

13. Leonard Feather, *Inside Jazz* (New York: Da Capo Press, 1977), p. 24.

14. Kernfield, p. 428.

15. Berendt, p. 94.

16. Feather, *Inside Jazz*, p. 34.

17. Lyons and Perlo, p. 221.

18. John Fordham, *Jazz*, (New York: Dorling Kindersley, 1993), p. 112.

19. Dizzy Gillespie (with Al Fraser), *To Be, or Not . . . To Bop* (Garden City, N.Y.: Doubleday & Company, Inc., 1979), p. xii.

20. Ibid., p. xiii.

21. Ibid., p. xi.

22. Fordham, p. 113.

23. Berendt, p. 97.

24. Kernfield, p. 429.

25. Gillespie, p. 441.

26. Ibid., p. 460.

27. Ibid., pp. 527–529.

28. Carr, et al., p. 236.

29. Ibid., p. 236.

Chapter 7. Charles Christopher Parker, Jr.: "Bird"

1. Leonard Feather, *From Satchmo to Miles* (New York: Stein and Day, 1972), p. 133.

2. Gary Giddins, *Celebrating Bird: The Triumph of Charlie Parker* (New York: Beech Tree Books, 1987), p. 26.

3. Robert George Reisner, *Bird: The Legend of Charlie Parker* (New York: Citadel Press, 1962), p. 238.

4. Giddins, p. 36.

5. Ibid.

6. Barry Kernfield, ed., *New Grove Dictionary of Jazz*, vol. 1 (London: Macmillan Press, Ltd., 1988), p. 287.

7. Giddins, p. 28.

8. Leonard Feather, *Inside Jazz* (New York: Da Capo Press, 1977), p. 11.

9. Joachim Berendt, *The Jazz Book: From Ragtime to Fusion and Beyond*, sixth edition, revised by Gunther Huesmann (Brooklyn, N.Y.: Lawrence Hill Books, 1991), p. 91.

10. Ron David, *Jazz for Beginners* (New York: Writers and Readers Publishing, Inc., 1995), pp. 117, 118.

11. Ibid.

12. Giddins, p. 38.

13. Ibid., p. 58.

14. David, p. 118.

15. Berendt, pp. 90–91.

16. Giddins, p. 71

17. Reisner, p. 240.

18. Ibid.

19. Giddins, p. 119.

20. Giddins, p. 20.

Chapter 8. Miles Dewey Davis, III: "The Phoenix of Jazz"

1. Miles Davis with Quincy Troupe, *Miles: The Autobiography of Miles Davis* (New York: Simon & Schuster, 1989), p. 23.

2. Ibid., p. 20.

3. Ibid.

4. Jack Chambers, *Milestones I: The Music and Times*

of Miles Davis to 1960 (New York: William Morrow, Inc., 1983), p. 12.

5. Davis, p. 23; Leonard Feather, *The Jazz Years: Earwitness to an Era* (New York: Da Capo Press, 1987), p. 118.

6. Leonard Feather, *From Satchmo to Miles* (New York: Stein and Day, 1972), p. 229.

7. Davis, pp. 26, 27.

8. Ibid., p. 16.

9. Daryl Long, *Miles Davis for Beginners* (New York: Readers and Writers Publishing, Inc., 1992), p. 15.

10. Ibid., p. 21.

11. Leonard Feather, *The Encyclopedia of Jazz* (New York: Da Capo Press, 1960), p. 176.

12. John Fordham, *Jazz* (New York: Dorling Kindersley, 1993), p. 114.

13. Davis, p. 73.

14. Ian Carr, Digby Fairweather, and Brian Priestley, *Jazz: The Rough Guide* (London: Rough Guides, Ltd., 1995), p. 158.

15. Fordham, p. 36.

16. Davis, p. 170.

17. Barry Kernfield, ed., *New Grove Dictionary of Jazz*, vol. 1, (London: Macmillan Press, Ltd., 1988), p. 271.

18. Carr, Fairweather, and Priestly, p. 158.

19. Fordham, p. 114.

20. Davis, p. 333.

21. Joachim Berendt, *The Jazz Book: From Ragtime to Fusion and Beyond*, sixth edition, revised by Gunther Huesmann (Brooklyn, N.Y.: Lawrence Hill Books, 1991), p. 108.

22. Ibid., p. 107.

23. Ibid.

24. Williams, p. 180.

25. Long, p. 108.
26. Ibid.

Chapter 9. John Coltrane: "Trane"
1. J.C. Thomas, *Chasin' the Trane* (New York: Doubleday & Company, Inc., 1975), p. 15.
2. Ibid., pp. 15, 16.
3. Len Lyons and Don Perlo, *Jazz Portraits* (New York: William Morrow, Inc., 1989), p. 139.
4. Eric Nisenson, *Ascension: John Coltrane and His Quest* (New York: St. Martin's Press, 1993), p. 6.
5. John Fraim, *Spirit Catcher: The Life and Art of John Coltrane* (West Liberty, Ohio: Greathouse, 1996), p. 15.
6. Thomas, p. 49.
7. Joachim Berendt, *The Jazz Book: From Ragtime to Fusion and Beyond*, sixth edition, revised by Gunther Huesmann (Brooklyn, N.Y.: Lawrence Hill Books, 1991), p. 113.
8. Fraim, p. 34.
9. Berendt, p. 117.
10. Grover Sales, *Jazz: America's Classical Music* (New York: Da Capo Press, Inc.,1992), p. 194.
11. John Fordham, *Jazz* (New York: Dorling Kindersley, 1993), p. 120.
12. Ian Carr, Digby Fairweather, and Brian Priestley, *Jazz: The Rough Guide* (London: Rough Guides, Ltd., 1995), p. 132.
13. Berendt, p. 116.
14, Fordham, p. 120.
15. Leonard Feather, *The Encyclopedia of Jazz* (New York: Da Capo Press, 1960), p. 167.
16. Fordham, p. 120.
17. Sales, p. 196.

Chapter 10. Wynton Marsalis: "Back to the Future"

1. Thomas Sancton, "Horns of Plenty," *Time*, October 22, 1990, p. 67.

2. Ibid.

3. Ian Carr, Digby Fairweather, and Brian Priestley, *Jazz: The Rough Guide* (London: Rough Guides, Ltd., 1995), p. 411.

4. Barry Kernfield, ed., *New Grove Dictionary of Jazz*, vol. 1 (London: Macmillan Press, Ltd., 1988), p. 85.

5. Joachim Berendt, *The Jazz Book: From Ragtime to Fusion and Beyond*, sixth edition, revised by Gunther Huesmann (Brooklyn, N.Y.: Lawrence Hill Books, 1991), p. 138.

6. Len Lyons and Don Perlo, *Jazz Portraits* (New York: William Morrow, Inc., 1989), p. 358.

7. Berendt, p. 138.

8. Carr, Fairweather, and Priestley, p. 411.

9. Ibid.

10. Ibid.

11. Leonard Feather, *The Encyclopedia of Jazz* (New York: Da Capo Press, 1960), p. 411.

12. Carr, Fairweather, and Priestley, p. 411.

13. Kernfield, p. 85.

14. Berendt, p. 139.

15. Lyons and Perlo, p. 358.

16. Carr, Fairweather, and Priestley, p. 411.

17. Ibid.

18. Berendt, p. 140.

19. Carr, Fairweather, and Priestley, p. 411.

20. Berendt, p. 141.

21. John Fordham, *Jazz* (New York: Dorling Kindersley, 1993), p. 50.

22. Carr, Fairweather, and Priestley, p. 412.

23. Art Lange in Frank Alkyer, ed., *Downbeat: 60 Years of Jazz* (Milwaukee: Hal Leonard Corp., 1995), p. 188.

24. Lange, p. 230.

25. Carr, Fairweather, and Priestley, p. 412.

26. Ibid.

27. Lange, p. 231.

28. Carr, Fairweather, and Priestley, p. 412.

29. Ibid.

30. Berendt, p. 226.

Further Reading

Alkyer, Frank. *Downbeat: 60 Years of Jazz.* Milwaukee, Wis.: Hal Leonard Corp., 1995.

Armstrong, Louis. *Satchmo: My Life in New Orleans.* New York: Prentice Hall, 1954.

Berendt, Joachim. *The Jazz Book: From Ragtime to Fusion and Beyond.* Sixth edition. Revised by Gunther Huesmann. Brooklyn, N.Y.: Lawrence Hill Books, 1991.

Brown, Sanford. *Louis Armstrong: Singing, Swinging Satchmo.* Danbury, Conn.: Franklin Watts, Inc., 1993.

Carr, Ian, Fairweather, Digby & Priestley, Brian. *Jazz: The Rough Guide.* London: Rough Guides, Ltd., 1995.

Collier, James L. *Duke Ellington.* New York: Oxford Press, 1977.

Cook, Richard & Brian Morton. *The Penguin Guide to Jazz on Compact Disc.* Third Edition. New York: Penguin Books USA, Inc., 1996.

Crisp, George. *Miles Davis.* Danbury, Conn.: Franklin Watts, Inc., 1997.

Curtis, Susan. *Dancing to a Black Man's Tune: A Life of Scott Joplin.* Columbia: University of Missouri Press, 1994.

David, Ron. *Jazz for Beginners.* New York: Writers and Readers Publishing, Inc., 1995.

Davis, Miles (with Quincy Troupe). *Miles: The Autobiography of Miles Davis.* New York: Simon & Schuster, 1989.

Ellington, D. *Music Is My Mistress* (Garden City, N.Y.: Doubleday, 1973).

Esposito, Tony, ed. *The Golden Era of the Big Bands.* Miami: Warner Brothers Publications, 1995.

Firestone, Ross. *Swing, Swing, Swing.* New York: W. W. Norton, 1993.

Fraim, John. *Spirit Catcher: The Life and Art of John Coltrane.* West Liberty, Ohio: The Greathouse Company, 1996.

Frankl, Ron. *Miles Davis: Musician.* Broomall, Pa.: Chelsea House Publishers, 1995.

Gillespie, Dizzy (with Al Fraser). *To Be, or Not . . . To Bop.* Garden City, N.Y.: Doubleday & Co., Inc., 1979.

Gourse, Leslie. *Dizzy Gillespie & the Birth of Bebop.* Old Tappan, N.J.: Simon & Schuster Children's, 1994.

———. *Madame Jazz.* New York: Oxford University Press, 1995.

Hasse, John E. *Beyond Category: The Life and Genius of Duke Ellington.* New York: Simon & Schuster, 1993.

McKissack, Patricia and Frederick. *Louis Armstrong: Jazz Musician.* Hillside, N.J.: Enslow Publishers, Inc., 1991.

Monceaux, Morgan. *Jazz.* New York: Alfred A. Knopf Books for Young Readers, 1994.

Nisenson, Eric. *Ascension: John Coltrane and His Quest.* New York: St. Martin's Press, 1993.

Old, Wendie C. *Duke Ellington: Giant of Jazz.* Springfield, N.J.: Enslow Publishers, Inc., 1996.

Orgill, Roxanne. *If I Only Had a Horn.* Boston: Houghton Mifflin Company, 1997.

Raschka, Chris. *Charlie Parker Played Bebop.* New York: Orchard Books, 1992.

Rattenbury, Ken. *Duke Ellington, Jazz Composer.* New Haven, Conn.: Yale University Press, 1990.

Simpkins, C. O. *Coltrane.* Baltimore: Black Classic Press, 1988.

Tucker, Mark. *Ellington: The Early Years.* Urbana: University of Illinois Press, 1991.

———. *The Duke Ellington Reader.* New York: Oxford, 1993.

Selected Discography

Scott Joplin

Scott Joplin 1916 Biograph 20060
Made when Joplin was very ill. He died in
1917. Joplin's music has been recorded by many
artists, including Louis Armstrong, Eubie Blake,
"Jelly Roll" Morton, Joshua Rifkin, and Thomas
"Fats" Waller.

Louis Armstrong

Louis Armstrong 1923–1931 Jazz Classics in
Digital Stereo RPCD 618
*Louis Armstrong and the Blues Singers
1924–1930* Affinity 1018-6
Features Louis Armstrong with some of the
great jazz vocalists, including Alberta Hunter
and Bessie Smith.
*From the Big Band to the All Stars
(1946–1956)* RCA Tribune ND 89279
Some of the artists accompanying Armstrong on
this disc are Edward "Kid" Ory, Jack Teagarden,
and Chick Webb.
Chicago Concert Columbia 471870-2
This recording features Armstrong singing
"Tenderly" and "Struttin' with Some Barbecue."
Mack the Knife Pablo 2310941

Duke Ellington

Black, Brown and Beige RCA Bluebird 86641
An essential disc for the Ellington collector.

The Complete Duke Ellington & His World Famous Orchestra Hindsight HBCD501
Some standards by the Duke along with some rare recordings.

Ellington at Newport Columbia 450986-2
Music by Ellington that changed the history of jazz.

. . . And His Mother Called Him Bill Bluebird ND 86287
Ellington's tribute to his arranger, the late Billy Strayhorn.

Second Sacred Concert Prestige P24045
Church music, a blend of jazz, classical, and black gospel music.

Mary Lou Williams

Mary Lou Williams, 1927–40 Classics 630

Mary Lou Williams, 1944 Classics 814

The Zodiac Suite Smithsonian Folkways SF CD40810
Mary Lou Williams is featured with the New York Philharmonic Orchestra.

Free Spirits Steeplechase SCCD 31043

Live at the Cookery Chiaroscuro CRD 146

Benny Goodman

The Birth of Swing (1935–1936) RCA Bluebird
ND90601
An excellent example of the early Benny
Goodman.

After You've Gone RCA Bluebird ND85631
Music by the Goodman Trio with Goodman
(clarinet), Lionel Hampton (vibraphone), Teddy
Wilson (piano), and Gene Krupa (drums).

Benny Goodman Plays Fletcher Henderson Hep
1038

Live at Carnegie Hall Columbia 450983-2
A recording of the history-making event in the
famous music hall.

Roll 'Em Vintage Jazz Classics VJC 1032-2

Dizzy Gillespie

Groovin' High Savoy SV-0152

The Complete RCA Victor Recordings Bluebird
66528-2

Dizzy Gillespie & His Big Band in Concert
GNP Crescendo GNPD 23

Birks Works Verve 527900-2
The recording of the band Gillespie took on the
State Department tour.

Round Midnight Verve 510088-2
Considered by many to be Dizzy's best record.

Charlie Parker

The Genius of Charlie Parker Savoy SV0103
Some music critics believe this record is the
greatest recording in modern jazz.

Bird: The Complete Charlie Parker on Verve
Verve 837141
A collection of ten CDs. The release of this
album marked the beginning of Parker's appeal
to the general public.

The Bird Returns Savoy SV 0155

Charlie Parker Jam Session Verve 833564
Bird appears with great saxophonists Benny
Carter and Johnny Hodges.

Bird and Fats—Live at Birdland Cool & Blue
C&B CD103

Miles Davis

Birth of the Cool Capitol CDP 792862

Miles Davis and the Modern Jazz Giants
Original Jazz Classics OJC 347

Milestones Columbia 460827
Considered a "must have" recording for the fans
of Davis.

Kind of Blue Columbia 460603
Generally considered one of the greatest jazz
albums ever recorded.

In a Silent Way Columbia 450982

John Coltrane

Giant Steps Atlantic 781337-2

This disc has been called Coltrane's most playable album. It was cut as a part of a fresh start made by the artist.

The Best of John Coltrane Atlantic 781366
Contains "Naima" and "My Favorite Things" among others.

The Gentle Side of John Coltrane Impulse! GRD107

A Love Supreme MCA DMCL 1648
Jazz critics consider this to be Coltrane's greatest album.

A John Coltrane Retrospective—The Impulse! Years Impulse! GRP 31192

Wynton Marsalis

Wynton Marsalis Columbia 468708
The first recording of the young jazz artist.

Fathers and Sons Columbia CK37574
A record featuring father Ellis (piano) and brother Branford (sax).

Mood Columbia 468712
This record, made while Marsalis was on leave of absence from the Jazz Messengers, demonstrates his talent.

The Majesty of the Blues Columbia 465129
A tribute to the music of New Orleans.

Blue Interlude Columbia 471635

Index